Stop Bad Overthinking

Simple Yet Effective Techniques to Cultivate a Calm and Peaceful Mind

Read Adam

Table of Contents

Introduction

Jessica sat at her desk, staring at the blank page in front of her. She was supposed to be completing a presentation for the Board of Directors, but her mind was racing with a thousand different thoughts and worries. She couldn't help but overthink every little thing in her life. From the smallest decisions, like what to order for lunch, to the bigger ones, like what she wanted to do with her future. It felt like her brain was always on overdrive, analyzing and dissecting every possible outcome until she was left feeling overwhelmed and paralyzed by indecision.

It wasn't always like this. Jessica used to be carefree and spontaneous, but something had changed over the past year. Maybe it was the pressure of starting a new job fresh out of college or the expectations her parents had for her future. Whatever the reason, Jessica couldn't shake the feeling that she was constantly on the verge of making a mistake. As she sat there, trying to force herself to focus on her presentation, she could feel the familiar tendrils of anxiety creeping in. What if the Board didn't approve of her presentation? What if they think she's incapable? What if this was the beginning of a downward spiral that would sabotage her entire career?

Her thoughts spiraled further and further out of control until she felt like she couldn't breathe. She knew she needed to find a way to quiet the chaos in her mind, but she didn't know where to start. Finally, she took a deep breath and closed her laptop. She knew she couldn't keep pushing herself like this. She needed help to address them all, one thought at a time.

Like Jessica, are you constantly caught in a cycle of overthinking, unable to silence the never-ending stream of thoughts racing through your mind? Do you find yourself dwelling on the past, worrying about the future, and second-guessing every decision you make? For instance, your sleep breaks to the blaring sound of your alarm ringing, and before you can even open your eyes, you suddenly catch a train of thought that you battled so hard to get rid of the night before. As these thoughts come rushing back, your anxiety kicks in, and suddenly, you begin to feel those uncomfortable, familiar lightning strikes in the pit of your stomach.

Your heart begins to beat faster, and your entire mood shifts into a depressive state as you replay those stubborn thoughts. As much as you try to fight it off, these thoughts always find their way back into your head. With each one passing through your mind, you begin to feel tired and drained out before you can even start your day. By the time you sit down to have your breakfast, you have probably experienced 50 different thoughts. Well, it's safe to say you're not crazy yet. There is a term for this tomfoolery, and it's called *overthinking*.

With the dawn of each new morning, the day brings along with itself a sense of uncertainty amidst the certainty of what a normal day should look like. There is no plausible way for any of us to know how our day is going to turn out because we cannot see into the future. However, we still manage to fall into rumination over the past, present, and future all at once. Speaking of thoughts, what is the first one that comes to your mind when you hear the word *overthinking*? Do you wonder how thoughts could be measured? And if so, what would be the criteria to declare you have been overthinking? After all, we are but mere human beings prone to worry and obsess over a particular person, problem, or event, each of which has the ability to impact our lives positively or negatively.

Only an overthinker can truly understand what another overthinker is going through. The sleepless nights, the constant mood swings, the feeling of losing control, the fatigue, and the inability to be present at any moment throughout your day. The whole saga is just so exhausting that you can't even focus on what you need to. Overthinkers often question themselves on why they aren't good enough, and they can even go to the extent of reading emails and texts over and over or replaying conversations that have triggered their insecurities in their minds.

Overthinking does have the power to destroy your life, and it can push you into making decisions that aren't rational. It can take over your life to such an extent that you could lose everyone and everything dear to you. The reason you chose this book is because you are looking for a way to finally exorcise that overthinking demon that has been tormenting you for months, probably even years.

This is the perfect guide for you because this book is going to help you learn clever strategies aimed at overcoming overthinking. It will also help you keep your patterns of overthinking in check. In this book, we will explore the causes and consequences of overthinking and offer practical strategies for breaking free from this destructive habit. Join us on a journey toward greater mindfulness, peace of mind, and a more balanced approach to life. Are you ready to kick overthinking's behind? Let's go!

Chapter 1:

Understanding Overthinking

Overthinking is the art of creating problems that weren't there. –Taylor
Swift

Breaking Down the Concept of Overthinking

This chapter is aimed at helping you understand what
overthinking is and how it can manifest in different ways. Once
you are able to define overthinking and how it progresses, you
will be in a better position to take action against it. You cannot
find a solution to a problem you haven't identified, so allow
this chapter to educate you.

Overthinking Explained

Overthinking has been around for centuries! It is only recently
that people have started talking about their struggles with it.
People are no longer ashamed or discouraged to talk about how
their overthinking disrupts their everyday lives. Social media
platforms have helped bring awareness to this anxiety-fueled
condition; however, there are people who don't understand
what overthinking is. Let's break it down below:

- *Overthinking* is a term used to describe "the act of dwelling on thoughts or situations excessively, often to an unproductive extent. It involves constant analyzing, replaying, and dissecting of past events or hypothetical future scenarios, typically leading to heightened levels of anxiety, stress, and worry."

- People who overthink tend to obsessively focus on small details, and they also second-guess their decisions. They struggle to make choices because they are constantly weighing every possible outcome before making a decision. This can hinder their ability to relax, make clear decisions, or move forward in life.

- Overthinking is one of the most common cognitive distortions and can be a symptom of anxiety disorders or OCD. It can also be triggered by high levels of stress, feeling insecure, or unresolved emotional issues (e.g., trauma, PTSD).

Believe it or not, chronic overthinking is prevalent among youngsters aged between 25 and 35—73%—along with people aged between 45 and 55—52% (Acosta, 2022). It has become a growing concern, with more and more people falling prey to the endless cycle of overthinking.

Types of Overthinking

Aha, I know what you're probably wondering. How can there be different types of overthinking? Is it possible to think in different ways? Well, the answer is yes! Overthinking can manifest in various ways and impact individuals differently. Not everyone is the same, and we all deal with different situations. Hence, our overthinking would be different as well. Let's explore the various types of overthinking below.

Catastrophizing

This type of overthinking involves constantly imagining worst-case scenarios and excessively worrying about all the possible negative outcomes of a situation. This can lead to increased anxiety and stress. Let's get back to the scenario that was mentioned in the introduction to help you understand catastrophizing overthinking more clearly:

- **Scenario:** Jessica is preparing for a big presentation at work. She begins to worry excessively about the presentation, imagining everything that could go wrong.

- **Her thoughts:** *What if I mess up my lines and embarrass myself in front of everyone? They'll all think I'm incompetent, and I'll never be taken seriously at work. Maybe I'll even get fired for this. My whole career will be ruined because of one mistake. I'll never be able to recover from this. What if no one ever respects me again because of this one presentation?*

When this type of overthinking occurs, it can cause crippling anxiety, which makes it very hard for an individual to complete the task at hand. For the person experiencing this, it can feel like their entire life depends on the success of that particular task. If they fail at that task, for whatever reason, it would destroy a big part of their self-confidence.

Ruminating

Ruminating involves "repeatedly going over past events or conversations in one's mind, often with a focus on negative aspects or mistakes. This can prevent individuals from moving on and can lead to feelings of guilt or regret." Let's go through the scenario presented below:

- **Scenario:** Allister has just gone through a bad breakup. He had been dating Marcella for a year and wasn't expecting the sudden end of their relationship.

- **His thoughts:** *Was there something I could have done differently in the relationship? Why did she have to break up with me? I don't think I will ever be able to move on with anyone else. I invested a year of my life into this relationship, and now all that time feels like a waste. How could she break my trust after everything I did for her?*

Rumination makes it very difficult for a person to move forward in their life after a certain incident or event occurs, which is usually traumatizing in some way or another. This hurt, shock, or pain takes an individual by surprise and causes a great deal of confusion in their mind. As a result, they spend countless hours trying to make sense of their past by constantly replaying the same thoughts over and over in their head.

Analysis Paralysis

This type of overthinking involves getting stuck in a cycle of indecision and overanalyzing every possible option or outcome. This can make it difficult for individuals to make simple decisions and can lead to feelings of overwhelm. They may spend months researching different options, weighing the pros and cons of each choice, and seeking advice from multiple sources. However, they may become so overwhelmed by the volume of information and possibilities that they are unable to make a decision. Here is a scenario:

- **Scenario:** Charlene is weeks away from getting married to her long-term boyfriend of three years. Although she had said yes when her boyfriend proposed, she has been caught up in a web of overthinking ever since. When it comes to planning the wedding, she just cannot decide on anything.

- **Her thoughts:** *Am I making the right decision by marrying this man? Will I find a better wedding dress online, or should I go to a store? I don't think I should have a church wedding, although it would be something our parents would want. I cannot seem to decide on anything; maybe I should just call off the wedding.*

With this type of overthinking, people may find themselves frustrated and disappointed easily. Because of their inability to make a decision and stick with it, they tend to become overwhelmed to the point where they drop everything. This can be detrimental to their lives as it could impact their relationships, careers, and mental well-being.

Perfectionism

Perfectionism is "a type of overthinking that involves setting unrealistically high standards for oneself and constantly striving for flawlessness. This is one of the most common types of overthinking, and it affects a lot of young people." Perfectionism can lead to excessive overthinking about how to meet those standards you set for yourself in your mind, and as a result, it can produce feelings of inadequacy or self-criticism. Let's explore a scenario below:

- **Scenario:** Kevin is a first-year college student who has been a high achiever his entire life. He always scored A's in high school, and he plans on excelling in his college career as well. However, Kevin puts a lot of pressure on himself, especially when it comes to studying. He hardly goes out with his friends because he wants to spend as much time studying as possible.

- **His thoughts:** *I have to excel in college exams this year. I cannot get anything less than 90% for every paper, or else I will feel incompetent. If I go out with my friends, I will mess up my study schedule. I had created a study schedule for myself, and I have to follow it religiously if I want to obtain perfect grades.*

This type of overthinking pushes a person to live in a state of perfectionism at all times. Whether in their relationships, career, home life, or within themselves, it can lead to high levels of frustration and insecurity when things do not go the way they expect them to.

How Does Overthinking Develop?

It is true that overthinking doesn't develop overnight. There is a process involved by which an individual begins to grow patterns of overthinking that span over a period of time. It's also vital to understand that not every person has the tendency to overthink. There are people who do not linger on a particular situation or problem for prolonged periods. These people are able to move past the situation without overanalyzing and overthinking every detail. However, when it comes to overthinkers, they spend a lot of time trying to make sense of things because they have developed overthinking tendencies due to genetic, biological, and neurobiological factors. We will dive into each of these in more detail below to help you understand how overthinking is developed.

Genetic and Biological Factors

Research suggests that genetics play a role in the development of overthinking. Studies have shown that individuals with a family history of anxiety or mood disorders are more likely to experience symptoms of overthinking. For instance, an individual who has grown up with a parent who struggled with overthinking may develop similar traits, which fuels their anxiety and worsens their overthinking. Researchers also believe that genetic variations in neurotransmitters such as serotonin and dopamine, which are involved in regulating mood and stress responses, could contribute to the tendency to overthink (McGee, 2023).

Kangana's Story

Kangana was a young woman who had always struggled with overthinking. No matter what she faced in her life, she always spent a large amount of time stressing about it to the extent that she could not sleep well at night. This also impacted her appetite, and she would lose the desire to eat. It seemed like Kangana had inherited this trait from her mother, who was a chronic worrier and could never seem to turn off her racing thoughts. Growing up, Kangana had seen how much of a toll her mother's overthinking had taken on her mental health and relationships. Her dad left home when she was six years old, and her mother never truly healed from that heartbreak.

Kangana knew that she didn't want to be like her mother, but no matter how hard she tried, she couldn't seem to stop her mind from spinning out of control. As an adult, Kangana found herself constantly replaying past conversations, worrying about the future, and doubting her own decisions. It was a never-ending cycle of self-doubt and anxiety that left her feeling exhausted and drained. She was desperately trying not to become an unhappy and anxiety-ridden woman, but in that desperation, she unknowingly drew a path for herself down the same road she was trying so hard to avoid.

Neurological Factors

The brain plays a critical role in the development of overthinking. Studies have been conducted using neuroimaging techniques and have shown that individuals who overthink often have differences in brain structure and function compared to those who do not. As an example, people who overthink may have heightened activity in certain areas of the brain associated with worry and rumination. These areas are known as the prefrontal cortex and amygdala. Chemical messengers in the brain, also known as neurotransmitters, play a huge role in regulating mood, stress response, and cognitive function.

Imbalances occur within these neurotransmitters when an individual undergoes stress—overthinks—and certain chemicals are released as a result of this, such as serotonin, dopamine, and norepinephrine. These chemicals have been linked to conditions such as anxiety and depression, which are often associated with overthinking. In understanding the development of overthinking, it's important to recognize the complexity of genetics and biological factors at play. These factors may motivate individuals to overthink, but it's equally important to acknowledge the impact of environmental influences such as stress, trauma, and learned behaviors.

Psychological Factors

Apart from genetics and neurological factors, there are also psychological factors that play a role in producing overthinking individuals. Let's take a look at each of these factors in more detail.

Personality Traits Such as Perfectionism and Neuroticism

There are individuals who have a *perfectionist* type of personality whereby everything they do has to be done in a certain way in order for it to be deemed *perfect*. They will develop a picture in their head of how they expect something to turn out, and when it doesn't turn out the same, it causes frustration, disappointment, and anxiety, which promotes overthinking. It goes as far as to expect everyone else to do things the same way, and when things do not go as expected, they begin to overthink and obsess over it until it is done correctly.

Neuroticism is one of the big five personality traits used in psychology to describe and understand human personality. This personality trait is characterized by an individual being emotionally unstable, whereby they tend to worry excessively, are constantly anxious, experience frequent mood swings, and are prone to experiencing feelings of anger, fear, and sadness. When a person is neurotic, they have trouble controlling their emotions and often fall prey to their feelings. This leads to severe depression and anxiety, which makes the perfect environment for overthinking to fester.

Martin's Story

Martin was a man who had always been known for his sharp mind and attention to detail. His friends often joked that he overthought everything, but to him, it was simply a way of life.

He couldn't help but analyze every situation from every possible angle, constantly questioning his decisions and worrying about the outcomes. One day, Martin received an unexpected promotion at work. While most people would have been thrilled by the news, Martin's neurotic tendencies immediately kicked in. He began to obsess over all the ways he could fail in his new role, imagining worst-case scenarios and panicking about his ability to handle the increased responsibility.

As the days passed, Martin's overthinking only intensified. He found himself losing sleep, constantly second-guessing himself, and feeling paralyzed by his own fears. His friends and family tried to reassure him, but Martin's neuroticism had a tight grip on his mind, and he couldn't shake the feeling of impending doom. Eventually, Martin realized that his overthinking was causing more harm than good. He sought help from a therapist, who helped him develop coping strategies to manage his anxiety and negative thought patterns. With time and practice, Martin learned to challenge his overthinking and redirect his focus to more positive and productive thoughts.

Negative Thought Patterns and Low Self-Esteem

Millions of people around the world battle with their self-esteem. In this new age of social media, beauty and fame are the determining factors in how successful one is in life. Many people put on a front to show the world how confident they are in themselves, but when they are alone, the mask wears off, and cracks in their confidence begin to show. We all have experienced feelings of inadequacy and imperfection, be it in our relationships, careers, or talents. When we struggle with our self-esteem, it ignites a pattern of negative thinking that turns into a habit. The more time you spend focusing on your imperfections, the easier it will become to fall into the deep, dark hole of overthinking.

Having low self-esteem goes hand in hand with negative thought patterns. These two factors provide the ideal environment in which overthinking can be bred, and it all begins in the mind. Entertaining thoughts about how you aren't good enough will only make you feel worse about yourself. Yes, it can be extremely difficult to challenge those thoughts, but if you continue to allow them to dictate your life, they will only make you more and more miserable each day.

Lucinda's Story

Lucinda was a 25-year-old woman who had always struggled with her self-esteem. She often compared herself to others, always feeling like she never measured up to her own expectations. Negative thoughts filled her mind, telling her she wasn't smart enough, pretty enough, or capable enough to succeed. Despite her outward appearance of confidence, Lucinda felt like a fraud. She worked hard to excel in her career, but no amount of success could silence the critical voice in her head that told her she was worthless. Her relationships suffered as she pushed people away, convinced they would eventually see through her facade and leave her.

Despite having a stable life, a good job, and a loving family, Lucinda just didn't value herself as much as she needed to. She searched for fulfillment in all the wrong places by getting into meaningless relationships, partying often, and falling into alcohol addiction. No matter how hard Lucinda tried, she could not get those negative thoughts out of her head. Her overthinking pushed her to do things she never thought she would ever do. The feelings of inadequacy were just too painful for her to endure, all because of her overthinking.

Traumatic Experiences in the Past

Traumatic past experiences can cause overthinking in individuals as a way of coping with the emotional distress and negative impact the trauma has had on their lives. When someone has gone through a traumatic event, such as being involved in a car crash or becoming a victim of sexual and physical abuse, their brain can be rewired to be hypervigilant in order to protect themself from potential future harm. This can lead to constant rumination, analysis, and anxiety about the traumatic event and its consequences.

Overthinking may serve as a way in which an individual tries to make sense of their traumatic experience in an attempt to avoid similar situations that could occur in the future by regaining control over their lives. It can become a way of trying to process difficult emotions, memories, and triggers associated with the trauma, and this can be both exhausting and overwhelming. For example, individuals who develop PTSD as a result of their trauma often experience severe forms of overthinking that also impact their well-being.

Simmy's Story

Simmy, aged 33, was a vibrant and independent soul. She had a deep love for nature, art, and helping others. Simmy had a warm smile that could light up a room, but underneath her cheerful exterior, she carried a heavy burden. A few years ago, she experienced a traumatic event that changed her life forever. She was brutally attacked and raped by a stranger while walking home from work one evening. The assault left her physically injured and emotionally scarred, her sense of security shattered, and her trust in the world fractured.

In the aftermath of the assault, Simmy struggled to cope with overwhelming emotions of fear, shame, and self-blame. She became hypervigilant, haunted by flashbacks and nightmares of the traumatic event. Simple tasks like going outside or being alone became daunting challenges, triggering intense anxiety and panic attacks. Despite her resilient spirit, Simmy found herself overwhelmed by the symptoms of post-traumatic stress disorder (PTSD) that plagued her daily life. She isolated herself from loved ones, feeling unable to open up about her trauma or seek help. The weight of her pain and suffering grew heavier with each passing day, threatening to consume her.

Every night, Simmy would lie on her bed and think about how messed up her life had become. She would constantly think about how she had lost her sense of who she was, and it was eating her up from the inside. The trauma she endured left a mark on her psyche, and her mind became the most toxic place. Simmy cannot break out of her overthinking unless she finds a way to heal the internal wounds she still carries with her today.

Environmental and Situational Factors

Environmental and situational factors can significantly contribute to overthinking by creating conditions that trigger and fuel rumination, worry, and obsessive thoughts in individuals. These external influences can interact with internal vulnerabilities, such as past experiences, personality traits, or mental health conditions, to fuel patterns of overthinking. Here are a few examples of what environmental and situational factors contribute to overthinking:

• Societal pressure: Society often places its own expectations on people, and this unnecessary pressure gives rise to extreme waves of overthinking in individuals. Conforming to the standards of society is impossible because no one is perfect.

• Information overload: As the famous saying goes, too much of anything is never good for you. The same applies to using your mind too much. When you spend too much of your time thinking and taking in information, it can have an adverse effect on your mental health. You are not a robot, and your mind does need a break every so often. Not allowing your mind to rest and rejuvenate itself could lead to a mental breakdown.

• Social media: As previously mentioned, social media places unrealistic expectations on people, causing them to question themselves, their abilities, and their appearance. Watching strangers flaunt their expensive houses, fit bodies, and elaborate lifestyles on social media can be entertaining; however, it also triggers insecurities in those who are watching, and this sets the ball rolling on overthinking.

- High-stress jobs: It is possible for certain jobs to produce overthinking individuals. For instance, working as a lawyer, doctor, accountant, teacher, or paramedic. These are examples of stressful jobs that cause people to worry even outside of their workplace. There is a certain level of trauma that comes with these jobs, which also places a lot of mental strain on these individuals.

- Academic pressure: The pressure of excelling in academics is one that starts from a young age. Parents normally emphasize the importance of education as soon as their child is old enough to go to school, and they expect top achievers all around. This undue pressure of excelling and being the best can be damaging when certain lines are crossed and parents become too pushy.

- Fear of rejection: Rejection isn't always processed easily, especially when individuals are dealing with a history of rejection that has caused them pain. That pain and betrayal can stay with someone for years and eventually cause them to develop a fear of rejection, which also fuels overthinking.

- Transitions: When going through major life transitions like relocating, marriage, divorce, health issues, or losing a loved one, it can be extremely difficult to adjust without overthinking every little thing. For some people, going with the flow is simply out of the question. They will replay thoughts associated with their transition over and over until they finally happen.

- Narcissistic partner: Living with a narcissistic partner who gaslights you and makes you question everything is one of the most common reasons for overthinking. Narcissists have the ability to manipulate you and make you feel like everything is your fault. This leaves you in a space where you cannot make sense of what is happening in your life, so you replay every conversation and interaction in the hopes of gaining clarity.

Tyron's Story

Tyron, a 14-year-old boy, found himself grappling with the weight of peer pressure at school. The constant ridicule of his classmates, the subtle yet somewhat powerful influence of group dynamics, and the desire to fit in tugged at his thoughts, causing him to overthink every social interaction and decision he made.

As he walked the hallways of his school, Tyron couldn't shake off the feeling of being scrutinized and judged by his peers. The pressure to conform to certain behaviors, trends, and attitudes sat heavily on his young shoulders, leading him to second-guess his own values and beliefs. He knew what his parents taught him was right, yet those values didn't seem to fit with his friends. He often found himself hesitating before speaking up or standing out, fearing rejection or ridicule from his classmates.

In his mission to belong, Tyron began to overanalyze every aspect of his interactions with his peers. He would replay conversations in his mind, wondering if he had said the right thing or if others had perceived him in a certain way. The fear of making a misstep or being labeled as *different* consumed his thoughts, causing him to retreat into a shell of self-doubt and anxiety.

Despite his internal struggles, Tyron tried to put on a brave face and blend in with the crowd. He followed the latest trends, laughed at jokes that didn't resonate with him, and suppressed his true interests and passions in an effort to gain acceptance from his peers. Yet, deep down, he longed to embrace his authentic self and break free from the confines of peer pressure.

The Consequences of Overthinking

If overthinking was good for you, you wouldn't be reading this book right now. The truth is that uncontrolled overthinking is one of the major causes of anxiety and depression in people nowadays, and the longer it goes unnoticed, the greater the damage it will cause. Various consequences come with overthinking, and a lack of awareness is what keeps so many people stuck in an endless loop of self-torture. In this section, we take a look at the consequences of overthinking and how it impacts various aspects of life.

Mental Health Impact

Overthinking can really take a toll on our mental well-being in several ways. When we get caught up in our thoughts, it's easy to feel overwhelmed and stressed out, leading to increased anxiety. This can make it challenging to deal with everyday pressures and may leave us feeling emotionally drained. Sometimes, overthinking can cloud our judgment and make decision-making tough. We might find ourselves stuck in a loop of analyzing every possible scenario, which can breed indecision and a fear of making mistakes. When this happens, our mind becomes exhausted from being in a state of flight or fight. People who have experienced trauma begin to live their lives in survival mode, unable to move on from their experiences.

When there is an extreme amount of pressure on the mind, it will open doors to the development of mental health problems such as depression, multiple anxiety disorders, and stress. It becomes difficult to think clearly or make decisions when you are dealing with mental health issues. The amygdala—part of the brain responsible for regulating emotions and decision-making—becomes damaged as a result of prolonged stress and anxiety, and brain fog sets in. These mental health issues have a direct impact on your physical health.

Physical Health Impact

Overthinking doesn't just affect our mental health; it can also have physical effects on our bodies. Anxiety, depression, stress, and worry all have a negative effect on the physical well-being of individuals who are living with these problems. When we get caught up in a cycle of overthinking, our bodies can respond in various ways:

- **Muscle tension:** Overthinking can and will increase stress levels in our bodies, leading to muscle tension and stiffness, particularly in areas like the neck, shoulders, and back. This can cause discomfort, pain, and even headaches, which often become more severe with time.

- **Digestive issues:** The intense stress and pressure one experiences from overthinking can disrupt the digestive system, causing symptoms like stomach pain, bloating, indigestion, and changes in appetite. This is more prevalent in people with anxiety disorders. The connection between the brain and the gut means that our mental state can directly impact our digestive health.

- **Weakened immune system:** Chronic stress from overthinking can actually weaken the immune system, making us more susceptible to illnesses and infections. For people with autoimmune diseases (e.g., lupus, diabetes, psoriasis, multiple sclerosis), a weakened immune system can be a risk to their health. Prolonged stress can also slow down the body's healing processes.

- **Sleep disturbances:** Overthinking interferes with our ability to relax and fall asleep, leading to insomnia or disrupted sleep patterns. We could stay up past 12 a.m. thinking about everything under the sun. Poor sleep can further exacerbate stress levels and contribute to fatigue and brain fog, which can interfere with our work.

- **Cardiovascular problems:** Long-term chronic stress from overthinking and anxiety can have a negative impact on heart health. It causes high blood pressure, increased heart rate, and a higher risk of heart disease, particularly in those who have a history of heart problems.

- **Headaches and migraines:** The mental strain from overthinking can trigger headaches and migraines, especially tension headaches caused by muscle tightness and stress.

The physical effects of overthinking can really take a toll on our bodies in different ways, like causing muscle tension, digestive problems, weakened immunity, and cardiovascular issues. It's important to take care of both our minds and bodies to stay healthy. We can try incorporating some stress-relief techniques, getting regular exercise, eating well, and making sure to get enough rest to help combat the physical impact of overthinking. Our bodies will thank us for it!

Impact on Daily Life

As a non-overthinker, a typical day would look like waking up in the morning, getting ready for the day, having breakfast, and going about your business. You will catch up with friends and work colleagues and sail through the day effortlessly. Should something come up that causes you to become upset, you will feel those emotions but quickly return to your normal state of mind. For an overthinker, each day, there is a constant war inside their heads, and no matter how hard they try to go about having a normal day, they just can't seem to get their mind off things. When an overthinker wakes up in the morning, they already develop a frustrated and irritated mood because of the mixture of thoughts running through their mind.

If something upsetting happens in their day, an overthinker will harp on the events that took place, and they will replay every part of their day that led up to the event. This constant thinking significantly impacts an overthinker's ability to have a normal life. Once a habit is developed, it becomes difficult to break out of it, especially when you have been caught in the web of overthinking. Your days become filled with anxiety and overanalyzing, which only takes you away from enjoying the present moment. How can you appreciate life when your mind is constantly worried about the future?

Effect on Personal and Professional Relationships

The habit of overthinking can have a big impact on how we connect with others, both personally and professionally. It can affect how we communicate, make decisions, build trust, and take care of our overall well-being. Here are some ways that overthinking can show up in relationships:

- Communication warmth: Sometimes, overthinkers might find it a bit tricky to express their thoughts and emotions clearly. They might worry about how others will interpret their words, which can sometimes lead to misunderstandings or make it hard to have open and honest conversations.

- Building trust and closeness: Overthinking can sometimes make us feel insecure and doubtful, making it challenging to trust others fully. This can impact how close and intimate we feel with our partners, friends, or colleagues.

- Making decisions together: Those who tend to overthink might have a tough time making decisions, big or small. They often look at all the angles and possibilities, which can lead to feeling stuck and unsure. This uncertainty can be frustrating for everyone involved and slow down progress in relationships.

- Navigating conflict: Overthinkers may either try to avoid conflict altogether or dwell on past disagreements, creating tension that lingers. This cycle can lead to misunderstandings and hurt feelings, which can strain relationships over time.

- Emotions and well-being: Overthinking can take a toll on our emotional health, making us feel stressed, anxious, or having negative thoughts about ourselves. These feelings can spill over into how we interact with others, affecting the overall quality of our relationships.

- Performance at work: In a professional setting, overthinking can impact how well we work with others. Constantly questioning our decisions, analyzing tasks to the smallest detail, or doubting our abilities can slow down progress and teamwork.

- Feeling overwhelmed: The mental strain of overthinking can lead to feeling burnt out and exhausted. This can impact our ability to fully engage in personal relationships and meet our professional responsibilities, leading to a sense of dissatisfaction.

In the end, overthinking can create challenges in relationships, from communication issues to trust struggles, emotional distress, and a decrease in productivity. It's important for individuals who tend to overthink to practice self-care, reach out for support, and find healthy ways to manage their thoughts and emotions. This can help nurture strong and positive connections with others.

Advantages of Overthinking

Let's take a moment to appreciate how overthinking can actually be beneficial in certain instances. By carefully considering the different perspectives and possibilities, overthinkers often showcase their analytical skills and attention to detail. This thoughtful approach can lead to thorough problem-solving and decision-making, ultimately helping individuals to make more informed choices. Embracing the positive aspects of overthinking might just surprise you with the unique insights and solutions that can arise from this tendency. Let's take a look at the advantages of overthinking below.

Supercharged Problem-Solving Skills

When you find yourself overthinking, it can actually work wonders for sharpening your problem-solving skills in some pretty cool ways! Overthinkers dive deep into analyzing situations from different angles, paving the way for some seriously creative and effective solutions to tricky problems. Sometimes, overanalyzing certain situations can help you see things you wouldn't otherwise see. By diving into various perspectives and exploring different angles, your mind gets a great workout in understanding the nuances of a problem. This can help you come up with fresh and innovative solutions, possibly catching things that others might miss.

Moreover, when you really dive into the details of a problem, you uncover hidden complexities that could hold the key to a successful solution. And let's not forget how overthinking leads to a thoughtful evaluation of all your options. Taking the time to carefully weigh the pros and cons of different approaches sets you on the path to crafting smart, creative solutions to even the trickiest of problems. In the end, embracing your tendency to overthink can truly boost your problem-solving skills by nurturing a deeper, analytical approach, sparking creativity, and ensuring you consider all possibilities. It's like turning your overthinking into a superpower for tackling challenges with ease!

Attention to Detail on Point

Overthinkers have a meticulous eye for detail that ensures nothing escapes their sight, leading to thorough and incredibly precise work. Their commitment to excellence means that every task they undertake must meet a specific standard of perfection; anything less is simply not acceptable in their eyes. This dedication to detail extends to every aspect of their work, where every small element is carefully analyzed. Overthinkers understand that even the tiniest mistake can have significant consequences, so they leave no room for error. They take pride in their ability to identify and make right even the smallest of flaws, ensuring that their work is of the highest quality.

This relentless attention to detail speaks volumes not only of their pursuit of excellence but also of their desire to deliver outcomes that are well-executed and free from errors. By prioritizing precision and thoroughness in all their endeavors, overthinkers set a standard of performance that is consistently high and reflective of their meticulous approach to work.

Know Yourself, Know Thy Awesomeness

Through constant introspection and deep reflection, overthinkers develop a profound understanding of themselves, including their strengths, weaknesses, and values. This process of self-examination propels personal growth and development, as overthinkers are constantly seeking to improve themselves and evolve into the best version of themselves. Overthinkers have a natural tendency to analyze everything, including their own talents and capabilities. This self-awareness allows them to identify areas where they may have weaknesses or room for improvement. Instead of shying away from these weaknesses, overthinkers embrace them and view them as opportunities for growth.

Their obsessive nature drives them to work tirelessly on addressing their weaknesses, pushing themselves to learn new skills, develop new competencies, and overcome obstacles. By dedicating time and effort to self-improvement, overthinkers transform their weaknesses into strengths, ultimately enhancing their overall abilities and expanding their potential. This constant cycle of self-reflection, self-improvement, and personal growth is a defining characteristic of overthinkers.

Even though overthinking can sometimes feel like a bit much, embracing its perks can help you tap into your inner analytical genius and make some stellar decisions across various parts of your life! You can retain the *good* overthinking habits and get rid of the *bad* overthinking.

Segue

This chapter has helped shed some light on what overthinking is and how it can impact our lives both positively and negatively. Most people don't realize they have a problem with overthinking because they have spent a big part of their lives stuck in a maze of it.

Living life in survival mode as a result of the trauma you have experienced is detrimental to your mental health and physical well-being. Now that you have identified the signs of overthinking, and seen how it can steal your joy, peace, and appreciation for life, you will be able to take action against this chaotic habit. The next chapter will help you identify the patterns associated with overthinking so you can make a change before your overthinking gets the best of you.

Chapter 2:

Identifying Overthinking

Patterns

Overthinking is like quicksand; the more you struggle, the deeper you sink.
—Emily Dickenson

Unveiling the Triggers and Patterns Associated With Overthinking

In this chapter, we focus on shedding light on the triggers and patterns directly associated with overthinking. You will come to understand how the mind works and what triggers it to go on an overthinking binge. Once you identify the patterns, you will then be in a better position to tackle the problem head-on.

Joanie's Story

Joanie was a 35-year-old woman constantly plagued by a swarm of thoughts that seemed to never end. From the moment she woke up in the morning to the time she lay in bed at night, her mind raced with worries, doubts, and what-ifs. At work, Joanie found it difficult to focus on her tasks as she would often get lost in a maze of overthinking. She second-guessed her decisions all the time and rarely accepted help from anyone. Joanie developed a habit of replaying conversations in her head and worried about the future and all it entailed. She just couldn't handle it anymore. Her mind no longer belonged to her as she lost it to overthinking.

Despite noticing the negative impact of her overthinking, Joanie found it difficult to identify the patterns and break free from them. She tried mindfulness exercises, meditation, and journaling, but the thoughts continued to consume her. She couldn't understand where these thoughts came from or why she couldn't control them, but she knew she had to do some self-reflection to find the answers to her questions. If she wanted to change her life and break the hold overthinking had over her, Joanie had to put in the hard work required to set things right.

If Joanie understood her personal triggers, she would be able to have more control over her overthinking tendencies. This would also help her get rid of the patterns that have developed as a result of these triggers. It was difficult for Joanie to stay on track, especially since the problem was not in front of her but inside her mind. She knew that she had to help herself, and the only way she could do this was by educating herself on her triggers.

Recognizing the Signs of Overthinking

Overthinking is a silent creeper that camouflages itself as anxiety, frustration, stress, and worry. Overthinkers often believe this is a normal way of life, and the only way they can solve a problem is by thinking about every possible scenario. The habit of overthinking develops in childhood, a phase where it's hard to determine what is right and what is wrong. This is why overthinking slips through the cracks and goes on to become a way of life for many people. When this happens, it becomes all the more difficult to recognize the signs of overthinking on your own. In this section, we will highlight various signs associated with *analysis paralysis*, an important type of overthinking.

Common Characteristics of Overthinking

Let's begin with understanding what the common characteristics of overthinking are. For those of us who like to beat a dead horse, it's vital that we make ourselves aware of these characteristics. We will take a look at the top three characteristics that aren't difficult to identify. A nudge in the right direction will help you see the signs that are in plain sight.

Repetitiveness

Repetitiveness is a common characteristic of overthinking, often seen in the constant rumination and cycling of thoughts in one's mind. When someone is caught in the cycle of overthinking, they tend to get stuck in a pattern of repetitive thoughts where the same worries, doubts, and scenarios play on a loop in their mind. This repetitiveness can feel overwhelming and tiring as the individual struggles to break free from the cycle of overthinking. It can create a sense of feeling trapped in one's own thoughts, making it difficult to move past the loop of repetitive thinking patterns.

Moreover, the repetitive nature of overthinking can make decision-making and problem-solving more challenging, as the individual becomes fixated on the same thoughts and has difficulty seeing things from a fresh perspective. This can lead to increased stress, anxiety, and feelings of being inundated by constant mental chatter. In essence, repetitiveness is a significant aspect of overthinking that can impede one's ability to think clearly, make decisions, and find inner peace and balance. By acknowledging and addressing this pattern of repetitiveness, individuals can take positive steps toward breaking free from overthinking and fostering a healthier mindset.

No productiveness

No productiveness as a sign of overthinking reflects how individuals immersed in deep rumination and analysis can face challenges in moving forward or taking action. When caught up in overthinking, their thoughts often circle around in repetitive and sometimes unproductive patterns, holding them back in a cycle of analysis and concern without progressing toward a resolution or decision. This lack of productivity can show up in different ways. People may spend excessive time pondering potential outcomes or scenarios, leading to a feeling of being stuck and finding it hard to take the necessary steps. Overthinkers might also strive for perfection, meticulously examining details and seeking an impossible level of certainty before making a choice, hindering their progress.

Moreover, the mental energy and time invested in overthinking can detract from productivity and overall effectiveness in daily tasks. Overthinkers may struggle to focus, make decisions, or complete tasks efficiently, resulting in reduced productivity and a sense of dissatisfaction. Ultimately, recognizing no productiveness as a sign of overthinking sheds light on how excessive rumination can hinder an individual's ability to act, make decisions, and reach their goals. By acknowledging this pattern and developing strategies to manage overthinking, individuals can break free from unproductiveness and move toward a more proactive and balanced approach to thinking and living.

Negativity

Negativity often tends to show up as a prominent trait of overthinking because individuals in this mode have a habit of focusing on worst-case scenarios, possible problems, and perceived shortcomings. When caught in the overthinking cycle, these negative thoughts can get blown out of proportion, giving rise to a heightened sense of pessimism and self-criticism. In the midst of overthinking, people may find themselves dwelling on past mistakes, fixating on potential future setbacks, or engaging in self-doubt and negative self-talk. This continual rumination on the negative aspects of their lives can fuel emotions like anxiety, stress, and even feelings of low self-worth, creating a cycle where pessimistic thoughts reinforce one another.

Additionally, overthinkers may tend to catastrophize situations, painting vivid mental pictures of the worst possible outcomes and spinning elaborate tales of impending doom in their minds. This slide into negativity can cloud their judgment, making it difficult to see situations clearly and leading to a feeling of being overwhelmed and powerless. The presence of negativity in overthinking can also color how individuals view and engage with the world around them. They might interpret neutral or positive occurrences through a negative lens, skewing their perspective and fostering a general sense of dissatisfaction or gloom. It can be extremely challenging to find anything positive once negativity takes hold of your mindset.

Behavioral Indicators of Overthinking: Physical Signs

Not surprisingly, overthinking can show up in the physical aspect of your life, namely behavior and well-being. Since all the thinking is done in the mind, it doesn't take long to impact your body and health. Let's look at each aspect in more detail below.

Restlessness

Every overthinker knows the struggle with restlessness. No matter what you may be busy with at work, home, or school, your mind will not stay focused on the task at hand. It will wander off and become lost in the same thoughts over and over again. A big reason for an overthinker to become restless is that they are constantly analyzing and evaluating every situation and decision. This leads to feelings of overwhelm, anxiety, and confusion. This constant mental activity can prevent you from being able to relax or switch off your thoughts, leading to restlessness and difficulty in finding peace and tranquility. It becomes difficult to take in the present moment and give your all to the people around you. This restlessness sparks anxiety and keeps you in a constant state of fight-or-flight.

Insomnia

It's like having a warm cup of tea, cozy under a soft blanket when an overthinker's mind is a whirlwind of thoughts that just won't calm down. All those worries about the past, the future, and every little detail keep the brain buzzing and on high alert, making it nearly impossible to relax and drift off to sleep. This flurry of mental activity can lead to thoughts racing faster than a speeding train, a heart rate quicker than a drumbeat, and stress hormones like cortisol running rampant. No wonder it's hard for the overthinker to switch off and unwind, as sleep feels elusive and out of reach.

Not forgetting, the lack of quality rest can make things even trickier—it's like a never-ending loop of rumination and worry that only worsens the insomnia. How is it possible to fall asleep when your mind is chaotic, and your body is stuck in a fight-or-flight mode? In order for an individual to have a sound rest, their brain must send an instruction to the body, communicating the message that it's time to wind down and relax. If the mind is busy all the time, how can it communicate this message to the body? This occurs as a result of overthinking.

Fatigue

Fatigue is a symptom of overthinking that often indicates there is something you need to check up on. Spending all that time going in circles, thinking the same thoughts over and over, and being in a state of constant restlessness will definitely take a toll on the mind and body. If your mind and your body aren't getting enough rest, it's a given that fatigue will assuredly set it. It takes a lot of mental and physical strength to be an overthinker. This habit is not for the weak because it really takes a lot out of you.

Behavioral Indicators of Overthinking: Behavioral Signs

Along with the physical signs of overthinking, there are also behavioral signs that people must be aware of. Being an overthinker does impact your decision-making abilities, your ability to get things done, as well as your self-confidence. Let's dive deeper into these behavioral signs below.

Decision-Making

Overthinking, while natural at times, can sometimes get in the way of your ability to make wise decisions. It's easy to get caught up in a maze of overthinking when you believe there are endless possibilities and potential outcomes. This may cause you to become confused about which way to turn. When you are confused about making simple decisions, you actually miss out on great opportunities because you become stuck in a loop of overthinking.

Moreover, overthinking can create brain fog, making it hard to see things clearly, as you may become overwhelmed by all the information circling around in your mind. When you don't see things clearly, you are at risk of making choices driven more by emotions than by reason, which may not always be the best path to take. On top of that, overthinking can bring on added stress and anxiety. Who can make good decisions in a state of anxiety? No one can. It might also make you doubt yourself and your abilities, which can shake your confidence when it comes to making choices.

Procrastination

Yes, some overthinkers are always focused on getting things done on time because of the stress and anxiety they experience when they have deadlines to meet. The thought of the due date approaching is enough to get an overthinker to finish their task well before that date just so they can end their anxiety around that particular task. On the other hand, there are people who become procrastinators as a result of their crippling overthinking. Once they become lost in their thoughts, they lose the desire to get things done because of the extreme anxiety they feel. The task at hand might cause them to overthink and lose confidence in themselves.

Additionally, when a person becomes stuck in a loop of overthinking, it cripples them to such an extent that they cannot even get out of bed. Avoiding a task or the issue at hand might seem easier than facing it head-on. This is how overthinkers end up procrastinating and avoiding important tasks. The world will still spin, and people will continue living, but an overthinker will remain stuck in that maze, delaying every aspect of their life until they are ready to face it.

Need for Constant Reassurance

Overthinkers often find comfort in seeking reassurance from others because their tendency to deeply analyze situations can sometimes leave them feeling unsure about their own decisions. By second-guessing themselves, they may seek validation from those they trust to feel more confident in their choices. Regular reassurance helps to provide them with a sense of validation and encouragement, guiding them in navigating their doubts and fears. The reality is that overthinkers may grapple with moments of self-doubt and low self-esteem, which can heighten their need for reassurance from their friends and family members to boost their confidence. Fearing mistakes or negative outcomes, overthinkers turn to others for validation to ease their worries.

The overthinker's constant need for reassurance might also be tied to a fear of failure or rejection. Seeking acceptance and approval from others helps overthinkers feel valued and secure, reinforcing their sense of self-worth. This can be particularly true for overthinkers in relationships. If their partner cannot provide constant reassurance, the overthinker will slowly move away from the relationship in the hopes of protecting themself from further pain. The smallest of misunderstandings could cause the biggest waves in a relationship with an overthinker, and once trust is questioned, an overthinker will always be on guard, needing constant reassurance to feel comfortable in the relationship.

Identifying Patterns in Thought Content

Melanie's Story

Melanie, a vibrant 25-year-old single mom, found herself struggling with the challenge of identifying the patterns of her overthinking. Juggling work, parenting, and personal aspirations, she often felt overwhelmed by the constant chatter inside her head. Despite her best efforts, Melanie found it difficult to settle the intrusive loops of analysis that would invade her mind, leaving her feeling drained and anxious. One of the breakthroughs for Melanie was the realization that she tended to cycle through the same worries and concerns, replaying them over and over again in her thoughts. Whether it was fretting about her daughter's well-being or stressing over her career prospects, she noticed that certain themes would consistently dominate her overactive mind. This awareness allowed her to recognize the common triggers that ignited her tendency to overthink, giving her a starting point for breaking the cycle.

To help her navigate through this journey, Melanie began keeping a thought journal. By jotting down her recurring worries and anxieties, she was able to identify patterns in her overthinking more clearly. This practice gave her a tangible record of her thoughts and allowed her to identify the common themes that fueled her overanalysis. Melanie also started incorporating mindfulness into her daily routine. This involved taking a moment to pause and observe her thoughts without judgment when she caught herself overthinking. Through this practice, Melanie was able to gain a greater awareness of the patterns in her thinking as well as recognize when she was getting caught up in overthinking.

How to Identify Patterns in Overthinking

If you're looking to spot patterns in your thoughts when you're overthinking, a great starting point is to simply tune in to your inner voice. When you are overthinking, you are basically having conversations with yourself internally. Pay attention and see if you catch yourself going round and round in circles of analysis. Take note of certain ideas or scenarios that keep popping up in your mind or if your thoughts start spiraling into worry or doubt. Another great idea is to keep a journal or diary of your thoughts. Jot down the recurring themes or topics that occupy your mind during those overthinking moments. It's like creating a roadmap that can help you pinpoint common patterns and triggers that fuel your tendency to overthink.

Experimenting with mindfulness and staying present in the current moment is also really helpful. When you realize you're overthinking, give yourself a pause and observe your thoughts without any harsh judgment. This gentle observation can help you tune in to the patterns in your thinking and recognize when you're slipping into overthinking mode. Keep a journal to record the observations you make about your thought patterns. This is an essential step toward taking control of your overthinking.

Interactive Element: Exercise to Identify Patterns in Overthinking

Below are a couple of questions you should ask yourself to help identify the patterns in your thought processes. Find a quiet place to complete this exercise, and ensure there are no distractions. Be honest in your answers, and aim to keep an open mind. It is only when we are honest with ourselves that we can truly help ourselves. Let's begin with the activity.

1. Do you regard yourself as an overthinker? If so, what makes you believe this?

_____

_____

_____

_____

_____

_____

2. What are some of the things you think about all the time?

_____

_____

_____

_____

_____

_____

_____

3. At what part of your day would you say your thoughts become more intense and difficult to control?

4. Do you become stuck on worrying about the same thing day in and day out?

5. When you meet someone new, do you find yourself thinking about them all the time? If so, what do you think about?

6. Are you easily triggered by things you see on TV, social media, songs, or people?

7. Have you encountered any trauma in your life? If yes, explain.

8. Do you find yourself relating everything that happens in your present to your trauma?

Based on your answers to these questions, you will be able to identify if there are patterns to your overthinking. It's vital to understand what your overthinking is all about and whether it is tied to certain people or events that have taken place in your life. There are people whose overthinking is a part of their personality, while there are others who developed overthinking as a result of a trauma that has occurred. Once you are able to identify your overthinking, you will be in a better position to address it.

Common Triggers of Your Overthinking

Overthinking is something many of us experience, and we often find ourselves going over our thoughts again and again. Sometimes, our overthinking leads to worry and anxiety. The triggers for overthinking are unique to each person and influenced by a mix of internal and external factors. By recognizing these triggers, we can start understanding our patterns of overthinking and find ways to ease its impact on our mental health and overall well-being. In this section, we'll dive into some common triggers of overthinking and chat about ways to address them thoughtfully.

External Triggers

External triggers of overthinking can include factors such as stressful events, criticism from others, or overwhelming workloads. These external triggers can lead to a heightened sense of pressure and self-doubt, causing individuals to ruminate and overanalyze. Let's take a look at some of these external triggers in more detail.

Work Stress

As mentioned in the previous chapter, the workplace can have a massive impact on your mental health. The pressure of meeting deadlines, the stress and frustration of working with others, and the lack of resources to get your job done are all triggers that set your circle of overthinking. For instance, you are required to work with a colleague who is very judgmental and criticizing on a project. This person always has something to say about the way you work, and now you are nervous about working with them. Criticism or negative feedback at work can fuel overthinking, causing you to dwell on your mistakes and question your abilities. This can trigger your overthinking and cause you to obsess over whether your work will be appreciated or not. If you are a perfectionist, your overthinking would revolve around getting things done the right way, according to what you deem as perfect. This cycle of overthinking could continue until you finish the project.

Along with stressing about getting this project done the right way, you will also feel the shift in your work-home life balance. Struggling to find a balance between work responsibilities and personal life can lead to overthinking the impact of work on overall well-being and relationships.

Relationship Issues

Being in a relationship can be stressful at times. This is because you are opening up yourself to someone and learning about them as a person as well. One thing people fail to realize is that when you are dating someone, you are two different people with different habits, mindsets, and personalities. Navigating through life with someone you are learning about isn't easy and can be challenging. There will be minor arguments and disagreements; however, these little fights can trigger overthinking. For instance, you and your partner decide to go watch a movie together. Before going into the cinema, you grab something to eat and notice your partner smiling a little at the cashier. Although you know it isn't a big deal, you can't help but feel insecure about it. This now triggers your overthinking, and although you choose not to say anything about it, it stays on your mind for hours. All through the movie, a million thoughts go through your mind, and you leave the cinema without remembering how the movie started or finished.

This is an example of how your overthinking can be triggered by something small that happens in a relationship, especially if you are dealing with trauma from your past relationships. If you have unhealed wounds, it will show up in your present relationships whenever your partner does something to trigger your memories.

Health Concerns

Health concerns have a way of nudging individuals toward overthinking, tapping into feelings of uncertainty, fear, and a sense of losing control. The smallest symptom could send you into an overthinking frenzy. Here are a few avenues through which health worries can lead to overthinking:

- Thinking the worst: When grappling with a health problem or symptom, it's common for thoughts to jump to worst-case scenarios, fostering excessive worry and anxiety. Body pains or headaches would turn into something serious in your mind, and the constant worry would cause more harm than good.

- Hypervigilance: Continuously scrutinizing bodily sensations and symptoms can heighten sensitivity, magnifying any perceived changes or discomfort and sparking overthinking. You'll always be on edge, waiting to see what other symptoms might show up, and this would leave you feeling restless and anxious.

- Research and reassurance-seeking: Immersing oneself in symptom and treatment research can lead to an overload of information and heightened anxiety as individuals seek answers to their health conditions in the hopes of finding solace.

- Memories: Past encounters with health challenges or traumas can reignite overthinking about current health worries, with individuals becoming attuned to potential symptoms or triggers. Understanding the difficult experience you once had, there is a fear of going through the same challenge another time around.

- Impact on daily life: Health concerns have the power to disrupt your daily routines and activities, increasing the time spent fretting over symptoms, treatments, and potential outcomes. Because your mind is so focused on your fears, it becomes hard to enjoy your present moment.

Major Life Changes

Life changes can act as catalysts for overthinking in individuals, primarily owing to the uncertainties, stresses, and disruptions that often come along with life's transitions. One way this manifests is through the uncertainty that arises concerning the future when faced with significant changes like relocating to a new city, embarking on a fresh job opportunity, or terminating a relationship. Such shifts introduce unknown variables and potential outcomes, motivating individuals to meticulously analyze various scenarios and potential consequences. Moreover, life changes can induce a sense of losing control over one's circumstances, stirring up feelings of helplessness as individuals strive to reestablish a semblance of stability amidst the whirlwind of change. The fear of the unfamiliar or unknown associated with life changes can further ramp up overthinking as individuals grapple with anticipating challenges, risks, and outcomes. Additionally, concerns about judgment or expectations from others can contribute to overthinking, as overthinkers fret over navigating social interactions or meeting societal standards.

Internal Triggers

Internal triggers of overthinking generally come from within an individual and stem from their insecurities and their inability to be optimistic about the future. These triggers of overthinking can be just as powerful and impactful as external factors in prompting individuals to dive into waves of excessive or repetitive thoughts. These internal motivators emerge from within the individual's own mind and emotions and can range from deep-seated insecurities and self-doubt to unresolved emotions and cognitive biases. Understanding and recognizing these internal triggers is crucial in managing and coping with overthinking patterns, as they can profoundly influence our mental and emotional well-being. By delving into the internal triggers of overthinking, we can gain insights into our thought processes, emotions, and behaviors, paving the way for more effective strategies to cultivate a healthier and more balanced mindset.

Feelings of Inadequacy

Everyone has their own fair share of insecurities that they keep hidden from the rest of the world. Most of our inadequacies stem from the fear of not being good enough. Some of us have failed despite trying so hard, be it at work or school, while others are in relationships with people who cheat and make them feel like they aren't enough. Whatever the reasons for these insecurities, they remain within people for years and are triggered whenever they see or hear something that reminds them of their pain. For example, a single mother has been raising her two children on her own since her partner passed away. The world is watching her, waiting for her to mess up. While she pushes on and tries to remain positive, there are days when her insecurities and fears get the best of her. She worries about the future of her children, their education, and their careers.

She feels she won't be able to give them a good education, and this could put their future in jeopardy. This mother stays up at night, worrying and thinking about what would happen if she couldn't fulfill her role as a mother. This is a classic example of how insecurities can trigger overthinking in people, robbing them of their sleep and peace of mind.

Need for Control

The need to be in control can spark overthinking in people by creating a constant internal dialogue focused on planning for every possible outcome. When individuals feel a strong need to be in control of their surroundings, circumstances, or relationships, they often become hypervigilant and focus their attention on potential circumstances that could rob them of their desired outcome. This constant monitoring and analysis can lead to overthinking as individuals strive to identify any perceived risks or uncertainties that could occur. Moreover, the fear of losing control can heighten the significance of minor decisions, leading to overanalysis and the inability to decide on something.

Additionally, the need to maintain control can create unrealistic expectations and standards for oneself, fueling perfectionism and self-criticism. This internal pressure to meet these high expectations can drive individuals to overthink their actions, choices, and behaviors in an attempt to maintain a sense of control and avoid failure or disappointment. The need to be in control can spark overthinking by encouraging worry, intensifying fears, and magnifying the perceived consequences of not being able to exert influence over one's environment or circumstances.

Mental Illness as a Trigger for Overthinking

Mental illness can act as a catalyst for overthinking as individuals grapple with cognitive distortions, intrusive thoughts, and heightened emotional reactivity commonly seen in psychological disorders. Those navigating conditions like anxiety disorders, depression, obsessive-compulsive disorder (OCD), or post-traumatic stress disorder (PTSD) may find themselves caught in loops of negative and repetitive thought patterns that feel overwhelming to navigate. For instance, anxiety disorders often showcase through excessive worry, catastrophizing, and heightened fear responses. This constant state of heightened alertness can push individuals into overthinking potential future threats, dwelling on worst-case scenarios, and struggling with decision-making due to the fear of negative outcomes. The deep feelings of unease and apprehension can perpetuate a cycle of overthinking as individuals seek to regain control or find certainty amidst uncertainty.

Similarly, depression can trigger overthinking by warping individuals' perceptions of themselves, others, and the world. Furthermore, negative self-talk, self-criticism, and a pessimistic outlook can fuel rumination on past mistakes, perceived failures, and bleak future possibilities. This ongoing loop of negative thoughts and beliefs can fuel overthinking as individuals strive to break free from the clutches of their depressive symptoms. Individuals with PTSD may wrestle with intrusive memories, flashbacks, and hypervigilance triggered by past traumatic experiences. The repeated reliving of trauma can ignite overthinking as individuals attempt to make sense of their memories, emotions, and reactions to triggers in their surroundings.

Overall, mental illness can serve as a trigger for overthinking by magnifying cognitive distortions, intrusive thoughts, and heightened emotional responses that make it challenging for individuals to regulate their thought patterns and emotions. Seeking professional support, engaging in therapy, considering medication, and embracing self-care strategies can all play crucial roles in managing mental health symptoms and easing overthinking tendencies. Remember, you are not alone on this journey.

Identifying Your Personal Triggers

Identifying personal triggers is the first thing one needs to do before trying the techniques to overcome overthinking. This is because when you know what triggers it, you know when and which techniques to use.

Identifying triggers entails:

- Self-awareness. You have to build self-awareness in order to pick up thought patterns and events that trigger overthinking. Notice when you're overthinking. Recognize the difference between problem-solving and rumination.

- Use tools like journals or checklists to track your thoughts and identify triggers. Maintain a daily journal where you record your thoughts, emotions, and any triggering events. Note down specific instances when you found yourself ruminating on past events or worrying excessively about the future. Checklists can help you document specific thoughts, the situation in which they arose, the emotions you felt, and the intensity of those emotions.

This will also help you start being more mindful and help you pick up patterns that you did not recognize previously.

Segue

This chapter has guided you in identifying your patterns of overthinking and understanding your triggers. You have come to learn about your internal and external triggers, and you have been taken through the behavioral indicators of overthinking. This information is crucial to you moving forward to the next step. Now that you have a deeper realization, we can move on to the techniques that will calm you and help you take control of your overthinking. Remember, your triggers are also tied to your insecurities and past trauma. So, unless you heal from what hurt you, it will be difficult to face your overthinking head-on.

Chapter 3:

Techniques to Help You

Overcome Your Bad

Overthinking

Don't let overthinking drown out the music of your life. –John Lennon

Tackling Overthinking Head-on

In this chapter, you will learn effective techniques that will help you tackle your bad overthinking. Now that you have a good understanding of what overthinking is and how it is triggered, you can take the next steps required to overcome the problem.

Lydia's Story

Lydia was a 32-year-old writer who had a talent for weaving words together to create beautiful stories. However, her gift often felt burdened by her tendency to overthink every detail. She would spend hours agonizing over a single sentence, second-guessing herself and struggling to move forward with her writing. One day, Lydia decided that enough was enough. She was tired of letting her overthinking hold her back from reaching her full potential as a writer. She began to explore different strategies to help her overcome this challenge.

She started by setting specific goals for her writing sessions, breaking down larger projects into smaller, more manageable tasks. This approach helped her focus on one step at a time rather than becoming overwhelmed by the project as a whole. Lydia also practiced mindfulness techniques to quiet her racing thoughts and bring her attention back to the present moment. Taking deep breaths, meditating, and going for walks in nature helped her clear her mind and approach her writing with a sense of calm and clarity.

On the other hand, Lydia made a conscious effort to challenge her negative self-talk and perfectionist tendencies. Instead of criticizing herself for every mistake or perceived flaw in her writing, she chose to embrace imperfection as a natural part of the creative process. As she continued to implement these strategies, she noticed a significant shift in her writing process. She felt more confident, focused, and inspired than ever before. By learning to tame her overthinking tendencies, Lydia was able to unlock her creativity and unleash her full potential as a writer.

Through perseverance and a willingness to change her mindset, Lydia successfully overcame her bad habit of overthinking and emerged as a stronger and more resilient writer. Her stories flowed more effortlessly, her words carried greater depth and meaning, and her confidence soared to new heights. Lydia had found the key to unlocking her true writing potential, and she was excited to see where her newfound clarity and creativity would take her next.

The Benefits of a Calm Mind

In the midst of the chaos of everyday life, try adding overthinking to the mix and see what happens. You'd instantly triple your chaos and magnify your anxiety to astronomical levels! Your mind would be a crazy place with you jumping from thought to thought, and I'm sure you'll agree that it can be exhausting to live life this way. Overthinking can get so bad sometimes that you wake up thinking deeply about something, go to bed thinking about it again, and, when your sleep breaks in the middle of the night, find yourself picking up right where you left off with your thoughts. When this happens, it becomes very difficult to go back to sleep, so you spend a few hours scrolling on your phone until you feel sleepy again.

This is in no shape or form an example of a calm mind. In fact, this doesn't even look like a healthy mind. People don't understand how important it is to have a sound, calm mind. Sometimes, overthinking may seem normal to a lot of people because they have been exposed to it growing up. In this case, they won't realize what a healthy mind should look like, and as a result, they will carry on with their patterns of overthinking well into old age. Below, we take a look at the benefits of having a calm mind.

Mental Health Benefits

- Reduced anxiety and stress: Less time spent ruminating means lower levels of anxiety and stress, leading to a more relaxed and calm state of mind.

- Improved mood: By minimizing negative thought patterns, you can experience an overall improvement in mood and emotional well-being.

- Enhanced mental clarity: Clearer thinking allows for better decision-making and problem-solving, reducing mental fatigue and confusion.

Emotional Benefits

- Increased emotional resilience: Learning to manage overthinking fosters greater emotional strength, making it easier to cope with life's challenges.

- Greater self-compassion: Reducing self-criticism and harsh judgment leads to a more compassionate and forgiving attitude toward oneself.

- Improved relationships: With less preoccupation and worry, you can be more present and engaged in your relationships, enhancing connection and communication.

Physical Health Benefits

- Better sleep: Decreasing overthinking can lead to improved sleep quality, as your mind is less likely to be racing at bedtime.

- Increased energy levels: With reduced mental strain, your overall energy levels can improve, making you feel more invigorated and active.

- Lower risk of physical health issues: Chronic stress and anxiety can contribute to physical health problems such as high blood pressure and heart disease. Overcoming overthinking can reduce these risks.

Productivity and Performance Benefits

- Enhanced focus and concentration: With fewer distractions from overthinking, you can concentrate better on tasks and projects, leading to increased productivity.

- Improved decision-making: Clearer thinking and reduced indecisiveness enable more effective and timely decisions.

- Greater creativity: A less cluttered mind can foster creativity and innovation as you are more open to new ideas and solutions.

Personal Growth and Development Benefits

- Boosted confidence: Overcoming overthinking can lead to greater self-confidence as you learn to trust your judgment and capabilities.

- More effective goal setting: With clearer thinking, you can set and pursue goals more effectively, leading to personal and professional growth.

- Increased satisfaction and fulfillment: By focusing on the present and engaging more fully in activities, you can derive greater satisfaction and fulfillment from life.

Social and Interpersonal Benefits

- Improved social interactions: Being less preoccupied with internal thoughts allows you to be more present in social situations, enhancing your interactions with others.

- Less anxious and stressed: The calmer your mind is, the more relaxed you will be. You won't feel anxious or stressed because of overthinking, and this will allow you to be more open and easygoing with people.

- You will not feel drained around people: Overthinkers tend to overthink more when they are around a lot of people, and this can be extremely exhausting. Once you have a calmer mind, you won't feel the need to question everything around you. You will feel energized and joyful after interacting with friends and family.

Jenna's Story

Jenna was a 44-year-old mom who had spent most of her life as an overthinker. She would analyze every situation, worry about every possible outcome, and constantly second-guess her decisions. This habit of overthinking had been with her for as long as she could remember, and it often left her feeling anxious and overwhelmed. Jenna couldn't focus on being a good mom because she was too busy criticizing everything she did as a mother. She always questioned her abilities and felt like she wasn't doing enough for her children. She would wake up feeling worthless and go to bed feeling just as bad.

One day, after a particularly stressful week of overthinking every little detail of her life, Jenna decided enough was enough. She realized that her constant worrying was not only exhausting but also keeping her from fully enjoying the present moment. She wanted to enjoy being a mom rather than feeling bad about herself and losing those precious moments with her babies. Determined to make a change, Jenna set out on a journey to quiet her overactive mind and find peace within herself. With time and dedication, Jenna began to notice a shift in her mindset. She found that she was able to approach challenges with a sense of calm and clarity rather than being consumed by anxiety and doubt.

As Jenna continued to cultivate a sense of mindfulness in her daily life, she began to reap the benefits of having a calm mind. She found that she was more patient with her children, more present in her interactions with others, and more able to appreciate the beauty of the world around her. Instead of ruminating on past mistakes or fretting about the future, Jenna learned to embrace the here and now with a sense of gratitude and acceptance. With her newfound sense of calm and clarity, Jenna felt a new taste of freedom and lightness. She no longer felt weighed down by the burden of overthinking but instead felt empowered to face life's challenges with grace and resilience. Jenna's transformation from an overthinker to someone who enjoyed the benefits of having a calm mind was a powerful reminder that it is never too late to change old habits and cultivate a sense of inner peace.

Mindfulness and Meditation

I'm sure you must have heard about the power of mindfulness before and how it can completely transform the human mind. But do you understand what mindfulness is and how it works? Well, *mindfulness* is "the practice of being fully present and engaged in the current moment without judging your thoughts or whatever is happening around you. It involves paying attention to your thoughts, feelings, and surroundings without becoming overly attached or reactive to them." Mindfulness is often associated with meditation and can help reduce stress, improve mental clarity, and enhance overall well-being. By practicing mindfulness, individuals can develop a greater sense of self-awareness and acceptance, leading to a more balanced and fulfilling life.

How Does Mindfulness Work?

You must be wondering how mindfulness works and what impact it has on your physical and mental well-being. If you haven't practiced this technique before, it all may seem very confusing to you at first. However, fear not! We will break it all down in this section. Let's explore the process of mindfulness and how it works.

- Breaking the cycle of overthinking: By focusing on the present, mindfulness helps interrupt the repetitive cycle of negative thoughts that characterize overthinking.

When you are mindful of your thoughts, you are able to stop them in their tracks before they become uncontrollable.

- Reducing reactivity: It increases awareness of emotional triggers, allowing for more thoughtful and less reactive responses. Being mindful puts you in a better position to identify your triggers, which means you can take action early to prevent these triggers from sending you into an episode of overthinking.

- Enhancing emotional regulation: It helps in recognizing and managing emotions effectively, leading to greater emotional stability. This is key to taking back ultimate control over your thoughts and emotions. When your mind is centered and alert, it provides the right environment to get the hard work done.

- Improving attention and focus: Regular mindfulness practice enhances concentration and the ability to stay on task, reducing distractions. This means you can now focus on what is important and get things done within the recommended time frame instead of procrastinating.

Lila and the Stranger

Lila was a curious and energetic child, always exploring every corner of her village and getting herself into all sorts of adventures. She loved taking walks in the forest as she found it captivating. One day, as Lila was wandering through the forest surrounding the village, she stumbled upon a wise old man sitting under a tree. The man had a serene expression on his face, and Lila couldn't help but be drawn to his peaceful presence.

"Hello, young one," the man greeted her with a gentle smile. "What brings you to this part of the forest today?"

Lila sat down beside the man and shared with him all her thoughts and worries. She spoke of her fears about the future, her regrets about the past, and her struggles with the present moment. The man listened attentively, nodding occasionally and offering words of wisdom.

"You see, Lila," the man began, "the key to finding peace and happiness lies in being mindful. Mindfulness is all about making yourself fully present in the moment, free from judgment or attachment to anything from the past or future. It is about observing your thoughts and emotions without getting swept away by them."

Intrigued by the man's words, Lila asked, "But how can I practice mindfulness in my daily life?"

The man smiled kindly and replied, "Mindfulness is like a muscle that you can strengthen with practice. Start by taking deep breaths and focusing on the sensations around you. Notice the rustling of the leaves, the warmth of the sun on your skin, and the gentle breeze on your face. Allow yourself to be fully immersed in the present moment."

Lila followed the man's advice and began incorporating mindfulness practices into her daily routine. She found moments of stillness and peace in her days. She became more compassionate toward herself and others, more accepting of life's ups and downs, and more grateful for the simple pleasures that surrounded her.

Years later, as an adult, Lila returned to the forest where she had first met the wise old sage. She sat under the same tree and closed her eyes, feeling the gentle whispers of the wind and the rustling of the leaves. In that moment, she realized that mindfulness had not only brought her peace and joy but had also unveiled the true beauty of life itself.

How to Practice Mindfulness

From the story above, you will gather how Lila took the stranger's advice and practiced mindfulness effortlessly in her routine. A simple explanation of just being aware of the present moment and everything happening in that moment is all you need to start being more mindful. Nevertheless, here are some tips to help you kick-start your journey to mindfulness:

1. **Mindful breathing:** Breathing exercises are incredible for practicing mindfulness. Here's how you can start: Focus on your breath. Pay attention to the feeling of air flowing in and out of your nostrils, or the movement of your chest as you breathe. If your mind starts to wander, simply guide your focus back to your breath.

2. **Body scan:** Scanning your body allows you to understand what you are feeling and where you are feeling it. You can do this exercise in the following way: Find a comfortable position either lying down or sitting. Close your eyes and focus on different areas of your body, beginning from your toes and working your way up to your head. Be aware of any sensations, tension, or discomfort without attempting to alter them in any way.

3. **Mindful observation:** Focusing on an object is an effective way of preparing yourself to be mindful. Here's how you can do this: Choose an object—like a flower or a piece of fruit—and observe it carefully.

Notice its colors, textures, shapes, and any other details. This assists in training your mind to focus on the present moment.

4. **Mindful walking:** Physical activity is great for clearing your mind, and one of the best ways you can do this is by taking a walk. Walk slowly and focus on the movement of your legs and feet. Notice how your feet feel as they touch the ground. Be aware of your surroundings, the sounds, and the sensations as you move. Listen to your body and be receptive to what you are feeling.

What Is Meditation?

Meditation is like a gentle hug for your mind, helping you find peace and clarity amidst life's busyness. It has been practiced for thousands of years and has amazing benefits for the mind, body, and spirit. Through mindfulness, deep breathing, and visualization, meditation guides you to a serene and balanced state of being. This ancient practice, cherished by diverse cultures like Hinduism, Buddhism, Taoism, and Jainism, has roots in the spiritual soils of ancient India. Over the centuries, meditation has blossomed into various techniques, each tradition weaving its own special thread of wisdom and insight.

Mindfulness and meditation go hand in hand, and they work wonders in calming an overstimulated mind and body. When you have too much going on in your head, it tends to show up in your actions as well. Meditation is well known for bringing peace and tranquility to chaotic and messy lives. It helps sort out the different emotions and thoughts you are experiencing all at once, and this brings clarity and stability to your being.

How Does Meditation Help With Overthinking?

Meditation is similar to mindfulness; thus, it has a similar impact on the mind and body. Although meditation is more focused on promoting relaxation and peace, it also kicks overthinking in the butt! Here's how meditation can help you calm your restless mind:

- Calming the mind: Meditation helps slow down the mind's activity, reducing the incessant stream of thoughts that characterize overthinking. This is achieved through various meditation exercises aimed at promoting tranquility. The more you meditate, the calmer your mind will become.

- Enhancing self-awareness: When you meditate, you are enhancing your ability to become more self-aware, which fosters a deeper understanding of your thought patterns and emotional responses.

- Promoting relaxation: Meditation is an incredible way to promote relaxation because it activates the body's relaxation response, reducing stress and anxiety. Nothing works quite like meditation, and this is why millions of people worldwide choose to set aside time every day to meditate.

- Improving mental resilience: Regular meditation practice builds resilience to stress and improves overall mental health. You cannot spend one hour a week meditating and expect to see results every day. There has to be consistency and dedication to your practice, especially if you are trying to create a new normal for yourself.

How to Practice Meditation

There are many ways to practice meditation, and there are various forms to choose from. Some people like breathing meditation, while others enjoy mantra meditation. It all depends on what works for you, and I guess you'll never know unless you try it! Below, we take a look at a few different forms of meditation that you can start with:

- **Basic meditation:** Embracing a regular practice of basic meditation has proven to melt away stress, sharpen your focus, and uplift your emotional well-being. It's like a nurturing friend who helps you cultivate a deep sense of tranquility and strength to navigate through life's ups and downs. In basic meditation, you find a cozy spot to sit or lie down, gently close your eyes, and tune into the present moment. You can choose to focus on your breath, softly repeat a calming mantra, or simply observe your thoughts as they dance in and out. The magic lies in staying relaxed and open-minded, letting distractions float by without holding on.

- **Guided meditation:** Imagine guided meditation as a gentle hand guiding you through a peaceful journey within. With the soothing voice of an instructor or a recording as your companion, you are led through visualizations, relaxation exercises, and mindfulness practices to help you unwind and connect with your inner calm. Picture yourself being gently led through a series of steps or enchanting imagery that encourages you to relax, center your thoughts, and nurture a deep sense of tranquility. The guide might suggest visualizing a serene setting, taking deep breaths, or releasing tension from your body, all aimed at helping you find your inner peace.

- **Loving-kindness meditation:** Embrace the heartwarming practice of loving-kindness meditation, also known as Metta meditation, where the focus is on nurturing feelings of compassion, love, and goodwill toward yourself and others. Through this beautiful meditation, you'll find solace in using phrases or mantras to channel well wishes and positive intentions toward yourself, loved ones, acquaintances, and even those with whom you may have challenging relationships. Picture yourself cocooned in feelings of warmth, kindness, and understanding as you embark on this journey of self-love and compassion toward all beings. By gently repeating affirmations like, "May I be happy, may I be healthy, may I be at peace," you'll gradually extend this circle of benevolence to embrace the world around you with genuine care and loving intentions.

- **Mantra meditation:** Embark on a soothing journey with mantra meditation, a practice where you gently repeat a specific word, phrase, or sound to guide your mind into a state of tranquility. Your chosen mantra becomes a beacon of focus, drawing your attention inward and gently nudging away distractions. Picture yourself settling into a cozy nook of quietude, closing your eyes, and embracing the gentle repetition of your chosen mantra. With each recitation, a harmonious rhythm unfolds, coaxing your mind into a peaceful space where clarity and serenity reign. This rhythmic chant paves the way for a serene, meditative state, allowing you to explore deeper realms of inner peace and spiritual enlightenment.

Practical Tips for Both Mindfulness and Meditation

- Begin with a small amount of time each day and then slowly extend the duration as you grow more at ease.

- Consistency is key: Practice regularly, ideally at the same time each day, to build a habit. Once you develop a habit, you will automatically incline yourself to meditate at a certain time every day.

- Be patient: You may notice progress becoming slow at first. Be patient with yourself and recognize that overthinking can take time to overcome.

- Create a routine: Incorporate mindfulness or meditation into your daily routine, such as during your morning routine or before bed.

- Use resources: Apps offer guided sessions that can help beginners get started and maintain their practice.

Cognitive Behavioral Therapy

Cognitive behavioral therapy (CBT) is "a popular and widely used therapeutic approach focused on improving the relationship between thoughts, feelings, and behaviors. It is based on the notion that our emotions and actions are influenced by our thoughts and beliefs about ourselves, others, and the world around us." By addressing and challenging negative or unhelpful thought patterns, CBT aims to help individuals develop healthier thinking and coping skills.

During a CBT session, a therapist will work with a client to identify and understand negative thought patterns that are often referred to as cognitive distortions. They also work on addressing behaviors or emotional responses that are triggered as a result. Through various techniques such as cognitive restructuring, behavioral activation, and problem-solving, individuals learn to reframe their thoughts and develop more adaptive ways of responding to life's challenges.

CBT is a nurturing approach widely applied to support individuals dealing with a spectrum of mental health challenges, including anxiety disorders, depression, phobias, and obsessive-compulsive disorder. This empowering therapeutic method also serves as a valuable resource for cultivating stress management skills, enhancing anger coping strategies, and fostering stronger interpersonal relationships. Furthermore, it offers a gentle pathway toward overcoming emotional hurdles, all within a short-term, goal-focused framework adorned with practical tools for managing and triumphing over psychological obstacles.

How CBT Can Help With Overthinking

Cognitive behavioral therapy is incredibly effective when it comes to taming your crazy overthinking. Here's how CBT calms your overactive mind:

- Identifying negative thought patterns: When you are experiencing those negative thoughts on replay, it's easy to become lost in them. This makes it harder for you to identify patterns in overthinking. CBT helps you recognize and understand any irrational or harmful thought that contributes to overthinking.

- Challenging and reframing thoughts: As an overthinker, you will understand how hard it is to reframe your thoughts, especially when you are caught up in a web of overthinking. When therapists use CBT, it allows them to question the validity of these thoughts and also replaces them with more balanced, realistic ones that are healthier and more productive.

- Behavioral activation: Overthinkers rarely step out of the house to do anything fun. They neglect their hobbies, interests, and passions, and as a result, they become withdrawn and unhappy. With CBT, you are encouraged to participate in activities that reduce stress and improve mood, breaking the cycle of overthinking and inactivity.

- Problem-solving skills: One of the most important things you learn in CBT is the skill to develop strategies that will help you address and resolve specific problems contributing to overthinking. This is incredibly essential to navigate the highs and lows of life so you can address trials with wisdom and optimism.

Best CBT Techniques for Overthinking

Cognitive Restructuring (Cognitive Reframing)

What It Is

Identifying and challenging negative and irrational thoughts to replace them with more balanced ones.

How It Works

By examining the evidence for and against a certain thought, individuals can see more clearly and reduce cognitive distortions.

How to Practice

1. Identify the thought: Notice when you are overthinking and write down the specific thoughts.

2. Examine the evidence: Evaluate the evidence supporting and contradicting the thought.

3. Reframe the thought: Develop a more balanced thought based on the evidence.

Example

Someone has the negative thought, *I always mess things up. I am a failure.* Through cognitive restructuring, a therapist would help the individual challenge the validity of this thought by asking for evidence to support it. They may then guide the individual to reframe the thought to a more balanced and realistic perspective, such as, *I have made mistakes in the past, but that doesn't define my worth or capability. I can learn from my past experiences and improve in the future.*

Thought Records

What It Is

A tool for tracking thoughts, feelings, and behaviors to understand and change patterns.

How It Works

By writing down situations that trigger overthinking, thoughts that arise, emotions felt, and alternative thoughts, individuals gain insight into their thinking patterns.

How to Practice

- Situation: Describe the context or event.

- Automatic thoughts: Note the immediate thoughts that come to mind.

- Emotions: Record the feelings and rate their intensity.

- Alternative thoughts: Write down more balanced, realistic thoughts.

- Outcome: Note any changes in emotion and behavior.

Example

Sitting down with a journal and writing about your thoughts regarding a certain problem or situation. In this journal, you will explain what the situation was and how it occurred. Also, record your thoughts about it and how the situation made you feel. Thereafter, write down a few balanced thoughts which have truth to them. Be aware of your feelings as you are doing this exercise.

Behavioral Experiments

What It Is

Testing the validity of negative thoughts through real-life experiments.

How It Works

By challenging and disproving irrational thoughts through evidence-based actions, individuals can alter their beliefs and reduce overthinking.

How to Practice

1. Identify a negative thought: Choose a thought that you want to test.

2. Design an experiment: Plan an action that will test the validity of the thought.

3. Conduct the experiment: Carry out the planned action.

4. Evaluate the results: Reflect on the outcome and what it says about the original thought.

Example

1. In a cozy and welcoming manner, imagine this: A lovely example of a behavioral experiment in cognitive behavioral therapy (CBT) involves exploring the belief: *I am always rejected by others*, by a certain individual.

2. Picture this: The individual plans a little experiment where they consciously engage in conversations and interactions with different people in various social settings. Throughout these interactions, they take note of their reactions, responses, and any moments of rejection. They might even keep a journal to jot down their observations and feelings during this exercise.

3. After these interactions and collecting all the data, the individual sits down with their therapist to review the outcomes together. Together, they dive deep into whether the experiences support the idea: *I am always rejected by others* or if there are instances that tell a different, more loving story. Through this behavioral experiment, the individual has a chance to explore the truth of their belief about always being rejected and perhaps discover evidence that paints a more colorful and kind picture.

Mindfulness-Based CBT (MBCT)

What It Is

Combines traditional CBT techniques with mindfulness practices.

How It Works

By cultivating awareness and acceptance of thoughts and feelings without judgment, MBCT helps reduce the impact of overthinking.

How to Practice

1. Mindful breathing: Focus on your breath to stay present.

2. Body scan: Focus your attention on the different parts of your body to keep yourself grounded.

3. Mindfulness meditation: Practice staying present and observing your thoughts without getting attached.

Example

CBT Mindfulness can be practiced by individuals under the guidance of their therapist. For example, a simple breathing exercise can help you find clarity and truth in your negative thoughts. As you sit in a quiet room, close your eyes and take in a deep breath. Shut out everything around you and just focus on your thoughts. With every thought that shows up in your head, make yourself aware of it and how it makes you feel. Don't push the thought aside if it makes you feel upset. Allow it to pass on its own, but understand where the thought comes from and if it has any truth to it or if it is just an aftermath of how you are feeling.

Decatastrophizing

What It Is

A technique to challenge and reduce exaggerated negative predictions.

How It Works

By evaluating the realistic probability of worst-case scenarios and considering more likely outcomes, individuals can reduce anxiety and overthinking.

How to Practice

1. Identify the catastrophic thought: Note the worst-case scenario you are imagining.

2. Evaluate the likelihood: Assess how probable this scenario is.

3. Consider alternatives: Think about more likely and less extreme outcomes.

4. Plan for contingencies: Develop a plan for how to cope with the worst-case scenario if it were to happen.

Example

Let's consider a situation where someone is experiencing the catastrophic thought, *If I fail this exam, my life is over.* The therapist would guide the individual through the following steps in the *decatastrophizing* exercise:

1. Identify the catastrophic thought: The individual acknowledges and expresses their fear that failing the exam would have devastating consequences.

2. Question the validity of the catastrophic thought: The therapist encourages the individual to consider the evidence supporting this catastrophic belief. They may ask questions such as, "What evidence do you have that failing the exam would truly mean your life is over?"

3. Explore alternative perspectives: The individual is prompted to consider more balanced and realistic outcomes of failing the exam. They might explore alternative ways to handle the situation and cope with the potential consequences.

4. Challenge and reframe the catastrophic thought: With the therapist, the individual works on reframing the catastrophic belief into a more rational and manageable perspective. For instance, they may reframe the thought to, *Failing this exam would be disappointing, but it doesn't define my worth or determine the course of my entire life. I can learn from this experience and explore other opportunities.*

Journaling Techniques

Journaling is one of the oldest forms of self-expression, alongside painting and drawing. It has made it to the modern age of technology and is still an effective way to sort through your thoughts and feelings. There are various forms of journaling one can use to help them curb their overthinking and bring balance to their thoughts. Believe it or not, journaling works wonders as it gives you the same satisfaction and peace of mind as a friend would. Let's take a look at the various forms of journaling below:

Stream of Consciousness Writing

What It Is

Writing continuously for a set period without worrying about grammar, spelling, or structure.

How It Works

- Clears the mind: Frees your mind from the clutter of continuous thoughts by getting them down on paper.

- Reveals patterns: Helps identify recurring themes and patterns in your thinking.

- Reduces stress: Acts as a mental release, reducing the pressure of unexpressed thoughts.

How to Practice

1. Set a timer: Allocate 10–15 minutes for uninterrupted writing.

2. Write freely: Don't stop to edit or censor your thoughts. Let them flow naturally.

3. Reflect: After writing, read through what you've written to gain insights into your thought patterns.

Gratitude Journaling

What It Is

Focusing on and writing down things you are grateful for.

How It Works

- Shifts focus: Redirects attention from negative thoughts to positive aspects of life.

- Improves mood: Regularly practicing gratitude can enhance overall happiness and well-being.

- Reduces overthinking: Focusing on positive elements reduces the tendency to dwell on negative thoughts.

How to Practice

1. Daily entries: Write down three to five things you are grateful for each day.

2. Be specific: Detail why you are grateful for each item to deepen the sense of appreciation.

3. Reflect on positive changes: Regularly review past entries to see how your perspective has shifted.

Cognitive Restructuring Journal

What It Is

A structured approach to challenge and reframe negative thoughts.

How It Works

- Identifies negative thoughts: Helps you recognize irrational or harmful thoughts.

- Promotes rational thinking: Encourages the development of more balanced and realistic thoughts.

- Reduces anxiety: By challenging negative thoughts, you can alleviate anxiety and overthinking.

How to Practice

1. Identify the thought: Write down the negative thought that is troubling you.

2. Examine evidence: List the evidence that supports and contradicts this thought.

3. Reframe the thought: Develop a more balanced perspective based on the evidence.

4. Outcome reflection: Note how this new perspective changes your feelings and behavior.

Problem-Solving Journal

What It Is

A method to systematically address and resolve specific issues that contribute to overthinking.

How It Works

- Clarifies issues: Helps you break down problems into manageable parts.

- Generates solutions: Encourages brainstorming of possible solutions.

- Reduces overwhelm: Provides a clear plan of action, reducing the feeling of being overwhelmed.

How to Practice

1. Define the problem: Clearly describe the issue you're facing.

2. Brainstorm solutions: List all possible solutions without judging them.

3. Evaluate options: Consider the pros and cons of each solution.

4. Create an action plan: Choose the best solution and outline the steps to implement it.

5. Review progress: Regularly update your journal with your progress and any adjustments needed.

Reflection and Insight Journal

What It Is

Reflecting on daily experiences to gain deeper insights into your thoughts and behaviors.

How It Works

- Enhances self-awareness: Helps you understand your reactions and thought patterns.

- Promotes learning: Encourages learning from daily experiences and mistakes.

- Fosters growth: Aids personal development by highlighting areas for improvement.

How to Practice

1. Daily reflection: Write about significant events and how they made you feel.

2. Analyze reactions: Reflect on why you reacted in certain ways and what you can learn from it.

3. Set intentions: Based on your reflections, set intentions or goals for future behavior.

Practical Tips for Effective Journaling

- Be consistent: Set aside a regular time each day for journaling.

- Create a comfortable environment: Choose a quiet, comfortable place where you can write without distractions.

- Be honest: Write truthfully about your thoughts and feelings to gain the most benefit.

- Use prompts: If you're stuck, use prompts to stimulate your writing (e.g., *What am I most worried about today?*).

- Review regularly: Periodically review your journal entries to track progress and gain new insights.

- Keep it private: Ensure your journal is a safe space for your thoughts by keeping it private.

Segue

Well done! You have made it to the end of another chapter. Your dedication to overcoming your bad overthinking is real. This chapter has helped you understand the different techniques used to control your racing mind. From CBT to journaling and mindfulness, you can try every technique to find what works best for you. In the next chapter, we focus on understanding long-term strategies that will help you combat your overthinking.

Chapter 4:

Long-Term Strategies for a

Calmer You

Overthinking is the art of creating problems where none exists. –Meghan
Markle

Finding Long-Term Solutions to Long-Term Problems

In this chapter, you will learn about various strategies that have been designed to help you fix your overthinking problems for good. There aren't any temporary fixes when it comes to setting yourself free from overthinking.

Why Are Long-Term Strategies Important for Overthinking?

Long-term strategies are often used for overcoming overthinking because they involve creating sustainable lifestyle changes and habits that can address the root causes of overthinking. Let's go back to our story about Jenna, a mother, from the previous chapter. Take a few minutes to think about what would have happened to Jenna if she hadn't learned long-term strategies to cope with her overthinking. She may have used short-term strategies to help her find peace in the present, but what would have happened in the long run? Jenna would have definitely fallen back into her habits of overthinking, and this time, it would have been more difficult to try again. Here are some reasons why long-term strategies are important:

- Building resilience: Long-term strategies help individuals build resilience and develop coping mechanisms that can help them better manage their thoughts and emotions over time. This can include practices such as meditation, mindfulness, and cognitive behavioral therapy, which can strengthen the mind and help individuals navigate challenging situations without spiraling into overthinking.

- Changing thought patterns: Overcoming overthinking often requires a shift in thinking patterns and beliefs that have become ingrained over time. Long-term strategies such as cognitive behavioral therapy (CBT) can help individuals identify and challenge negative thought patterns, replacing them with more balanced and realistic perspectives.

- Addressing underlying issues: Overthinking can be fueled by underlying issues such as anxiety, perfectionism, or low self-esteem. Long-term strategies allow individuals to explore and address these root causes, often with the help of a therapist or counselor, in order to create lasting changes in behavior and thought patterns.

- Cultivating self-awareness: Long-term strategies for overcoming overthinking often involve cultivating self-awareness and mindfulness, which can help individuals become more attuned to their thoughts and emotions. By developing a greater understanding of their mental processes, individuals can learn to identify when they are overthinking and take steps to refocus their attention.

- Promoting healthy habits: Long-term strategies often involve promoting healthy habits such as exercise, good nutrition, adequate sleep, and stress management techniques. These lifestyle changes can have a positive impact on mental health and overall well-being, reducing the likelihood of overthinking.

Overall, long-term strategies for overcoming overthinking are effective because they involve a holistic approach to mental health that addresses the underlying causes of overthinking and promotes sustainable changes in behavior and thought patterns. By committing to long-term strategies, individuals can develop the skills and resilience needed to manage overthinking and lead a more balanced and fulfilling life.

Building Emotional Resilience

When you hear the word resilience, what is the first thought that comes to your mind? Well, resilience can be compared to a tree, one that stands firm through every season without falling. Come winter with its blistering cold, summer with its scorching heat, autumn with its dryness and death, or spring with its torrential rains, that tree will stand upright through it all. Yes, the tree will sway from side to side, bend in different directions, and even wither, but it will always remain strong and sturdy. This is what resilience looks like—being able to go through any trial in life but bouncing back from it and staying strong.

Emotional resilience follows in similar footsteps. If you think clearly, you will realize a human being has seven primary emotions that all play a role in their life. These are anger, happiness, fear, surprise, disgust, sadness, and contempt. When we overthink, our emotions tend to run wild, leaving us with mixed feelings that are uncomfortable to handle. Sometimes, these emotions become too intense, and people begin to lose themselves to their feelings. Being emotionally resilient means that you are able to handle any emotion and adapt to the change in your feelings without losing yourself.

How Emotional Resilience Helps in Managing Overthinking

Being emotionally resilient has its advantages, especially when it comes to dealing with overthinking. When people become swept up in a whirlwind of thoughts, their resilience can help them stand firm long enough to overcome the storm. Here's how resilience works to combat overthinking:

- Adaptive coping mechanisms: Emotional resilience equips individuals with healthy coping strategies, reducing the tendency to engage in overthinking as a maladaptive response to stress.

- Reduced emotional reactivity: Resilient individuals manage their emotions better, preventing the escalation of worry and rumination that characterizes overthinking.

- Greater perspective: Resilience helps maintain a balanced perspective, making it easier to avoid the exaggerated negative thinking that fuels overthinking.

- Enhanced self-compassion: Resilient people tend to be more self-compassionate, reducing the self-criticism and doubt that often lead to overthinking.

The above points provide you with a brief overview of the benefits of emotional resilience and how it can aid in overcoming bad overthinking. Understanding the benefits is vital to move further along in your journey to setting yourself free from overthinking.

Emotional Regulation Techniques

Emotional regulation techniques are like gentle guides that support us in managing and harmonizing our emotions in a nurturing and constructive manner. They play a vital role in nurturing our mental well-being and cultivating positive connections with those around us. Through the practice of these techniques, we can skillfully navigate moments of stress, overcome obstacles with grace, and enhance the richness of our daily experiences. Let's delve into a variety of techniques designed to empower you in fostering emotional resilience and attaining a deeper understanding of your emotions:

- Deep breathing exercises: Learn and practice deep breathing techniques, such as diaphragmatic breathing or the 4-7-8 method, to calm the nervous system and manage stress.

- Grounding exercises: Engage in grounding techniques, such as the 5-4-3-2-1 exercise—identifying 5 things you see, 4 things you can touch, 3 things you hear, 2 things you smell, and 1 thing you taste—to stay connected to the present moment.

- Cognitive restructuring: CBT done regularly can help strengthen your mind and build layers of resilience that keep your emotions in line, especially when your thoughts are running amok inside your head.

- Challenging negative thoughts: Practice cognitive restructuring by identifying and challenging negative thought patterns. Replace these negative thoughts with more realistic ones and choose positive alternatives.

- Gratitude practice: Keep a gratitude journal, noting down things you are thankful for each day. This can shift your focus from what's wrong to what's right in your life.

- Embracing challenges: Look at challenges as real opportunities for you to grow rather than something perceived as a threat. This mindset can enhance your resilience by fostering a proactive and positive approach to difficulties.

- Learn from setbacks: Treat setbacks and failures as learning experiences. Reflect on what went wrong, what you can learn, and how you can improve in the future. Later on, we will discuss the setbacks in more detail.

Enhancing Problem-Solving Skills

Problem-solving involves actively seeking solutions to challenges with a goal-oriented approach, while overthinking refers to excessively dwelling on a problem without making progress toward a solution. While problem-solving can lead to effective outcomes and reduce stress, overthinking often leads to increased anxiety and the inability to decide. Striking a balance between problem-solving and overthinking is important for maintaining mental well-being and finding constructive resolutions to issues.

Overthinking often involves ruminating on problems without moving toward solutions. It's a repetitive focus on negative thoughts that leads to stress and anxiety. Reflection allows you to see the cause and effect of the problem, giving you an opportunity to learn from your mistakes so you can make better choices in the future.

Paralysis by Analysis

Overthinkers frequently get stuck in the analysis phase, unable to make decisions or take action, which exacerbates feelings of helplessness and frustration. Effective problem-solving skills can significantly reduce the tendency to overthink. They provide a structured approach to dealing with issues, helping to break down complex problems into manageable parts, thus reducing cognitive overload. Long-term strategies focus on honing these skills through practice.

How to Develop a Problem-Solving Mindset

An overthinker understands how challenging it can be to focus when trying to find solutions to problems as they arise. Your mind is already filled with complicated thoughts, which makes it all the more difficult to see a way out when you are met with a dilemma. Nevertheless, developing a problem-solving mindset is essential to navigate through the storms of life. Here are some tips to help you change your mindset into a problem-solving mindset:

Adopting a Proactive Approach

- Anticipate challenges: Cultivate the habit of foreseeing potential problems and preparing for them. This reduces the surprise element and equips you with preplanned solutions.

- Take initiative: Instead of waiting for problems to escalate, address them early. Proactivity reduces the buildup of stress and anxiety that fuel overthinking.

Cultivating Positivity and Optimism

- Positive outlook: Believe in your ability to solve problems. Optimism can reduce the anxiety associated with problem-solving and make it easier to find creative solutions.

- Growth mindset: Every challenge is an opportunity to learn and grow, and this is how your mindset should be. This change in mindset helps approach problems with curiosity rather than fear, reducing the tendency to overthink.

Encouraging Flexibility and Adaptability

- Be open to change: Understand that not all problems have a single solution. Being adaptable and open to various solutions prevents fixating on one approach and helps find the most effective resolution.

- Embrace uncertainty: Accept that uncertainty is part of life. Learning to tolerate ambiguity can reduce the need to overthink every possible outcome.

Building Confidence in Decision-Making

- Small decisions first: Start by making smaller decisions quickly to build confidence. This practice helps in reducing the fear associated with decision-making and overthinking.

- Learn from experience: Reflect on past decisions to understand what worked and what didn't. Use these insights to improve future problem-solving efforts.

Practical Problem-Solving Techniques

Along with developing a problem-solving mindset, it's necessary to also develop techniques that align with this type of mindset. The more you practice these techniques, the more inclined your thought process will become. Let's take a look at some of these techniques below.

Brainstorming

- Free-thinking sessions: Engage in sessions where you generate as many ideas as possible without judgment. This can be done individually or in a group. The goal is to produce a broad range of potential solutions.

- Convergent and divergent thinking: Divergent thinking is used to explore different possibilities, while convergent thinking is used to narrow down the best options.

Mind Mapping

- Visual organization: Create a mind map to visually organize information and ideas related to a problem. This helps see the connections and relationships between different aspects of the problem, facilitating a clearer path to solutions.

- Central problem node: Place the main problem in the center and branch out with potential solutions, resources, and related sub-issues.

The Five Whys Technique

- Root cause analysis: Ask "Why?" five times in succession to drill down into the root cause of a problem. This technique helps move beyond surface issues and identifies the underlying cause, making it easier to develop effective solutions.

- Example: If the problem is a missed deadline, the first "Why?" might reveal a delay in starting the project. The second "Why?" could show that initial instructions were unclear, and so on, until the root cause is identified.

SWOT Analysis—Strengths, Weaknesses, Opportunities, Threats: Comprehensive Evaluation

Use SWOT analysis to evaluate the internal and external factors affecting a problem. This technique provides a balanced view of what can be leveraged—strengths and opportunities—and what needs to be mitigated—weaknesses and threats.

Pros and Cons List

- Decision-making aid: Create a list of pros and cons for each potential solution. This helps evaluate the benefits and drawbacks of each option, facilitating more informed decision-making.

- Prioritize options: Weigh the pros and cons to prioritize the best course of action. This will give you a clear, direct path on which option is better to consider.

Improving Self-Esteem and Self-Compassion

Michael, a 16-year-old boy, often struggled with his self-confidence. With a sharp mind and a curious spirit, Michael was known for his intelligence and insight; however, behind his bright smile and friendly demeanor, he wrestled with a heavy burden: overthinking. From a young age, Michael had a tendency to overanalyze every situation, second-guessing himself and constantly worrying about what others thought of him. His mind was a whirlwind of doubt and self-criticism, leading him down a path of self-doubt and diminishing self-esteem.

As the years went by, Michael's overthinking only intensified, causing him to withdraw from social interactions and avoid new opportunities out of fear of failure. His once-confident voice became muted, drowned out by the relentless chatter of his anxious thoughts. One day, during a particularly challenging moment of self-doubt, Michael found an old journal tucked away in the corner of his room. Curious, he flipped through its tattered pages and came across a passage written by his younger self:

Believe in yourself, for you hold the power to create your own path and shape your destiny. Embrace your uniqueness and trust in your abilities, for within you lies the strength to soar beyond the confines of doubt.

Those words struck a chord deep within Michael's heart, igniting a spark of hope amidst the darkness of his overthinking mind. Inspired by his younger self's wisdom, he made a conscious decision to confront his inner demons and reclaim his lost self-esteem. With determination and perseverance, Michael began to challenge his negative thoughts and break free from the chains of overthinking that bound him for so long. He sought guidance from a supportive mentor who encouraged him to practice self-compassion and embrace imperfection as a part of growth.

As he embarked on this journey of self-discovery and healing, Michael discovered a newfound sense of confidence and resilience within himself. He learned to trust his instincts, speak his truth, and embrace his authentic self without fear of judgment. With each small victory over his overthinking tendencies, Michael's light began to shine brighter, illuminating the path toward self-acceptance and empowerment. He realized that self-esteem was not about being perfect but embracing his imperfections and celebrating his uniqueness.

Understanding Self-Esteem and Self-Compassion

People often overlook the importance of having positive self-esteem and a strong sense of self-compassion. One of the reasons why this happens is because they don't fully understand what self-esteem or self-compassion is. They often shy away from the things they don't understand rather than taking the initiative to learn about them. If you understood the benefits that come with having good self-esteem, you would work harder to ensure your self-confidence is in a healthy space. Here's a basic explanation of what self-compassion and healthy self-esteem are:

- High self-esteem is associated with positive outcomes such as resilience, happiness, and better mental health. When you have healthy self-esteem, you become more confident in yourself, especially when it comes to your skills and talents. There is no fear of not being good enough because you have faith in yourself. Low self-esteem, on the other hand, can contribute to issues like anxiety, depression, and overthinking.

- Self-compassion promotes emotional well-being by reducing self-criticism and enhancing resilience. When you have compassion for yourself, you are able to be patient and understanding with everything you are going through. This helps you manage stress and setbacks more effectively.

Now that you have an understanding of these two important traits, you can move forward to learn about developing effective strategies to boost your self-esteem. This is one of the important aspects of overcoming bad overthinking.

Strategies to Boost Self-Esteem

If it was that easy to boost our self-esteem, we would all be walking around with a bucketful of confidence. The truth is that we have to put in the hard work to ensure we teach ourselves how to give our self-confidence a boost each time it drops. Below, you will find some great tools designed to enhance your confidence in yourself.

Setting and Achieving Small Goals

- **Realistic goal setting:** Start with achievable, short-term goals that build confidence in yourself. As these goals are accomplished, gradually increase their complexity so that you attain a greater sense of fulfillment once you complete them. You'd be surprised as to how much this boosts your self-esteem. You can start by setting little goals, as this gets you into the habit of goal-setting. Once you have developed a habit, you can then move on to setting more complex goals for yourself.

- **Celebrating successes:** Acknowledge and celebrate every achievement, no matter how small. This reinforces a positive self-image and boosts self-esteem. Think of it as a reward for your dedication and hard work that went into making your goals a success. Celebrating your achievements with your friends and family boosts your self-esteem because you see how proud everyone is of your hard work. It also motivates you to continue setting goals and achieving them.

Positive Affirmations and Self-Talk

Speaking words of strength and positivity into your life is an absolute must, as it works with the universe to attract all things good. I understand that it can be difficult to say good things when you are feeling the exact opposite. If anything, when you are down, the only thing you'd want to do is vent about whatever it is you're going through. However, by shifting your focus to a more positive light, you can foster self-confidence daily. Here are some tips to help you use positive affirmations:

- **Affirmative statements:** Use positive affirmations to challenge and counteract negative self-beliefs. Statements like "I am capable" or "I deserve happiness" can shift self-perceptions.

- **Mindful self-talk:** Practice mindful self-talk by recognizing and replacing negative thoughts with supportive and encouraging ones.

Building Competence and Skills

Building skills is crucial for personal and professional development. Acquiring new skills helps individuals adapt to the ever-changing demands of the modern world and opens up new opportunities for growth and success. Whether it's learning a new language, mastering a technical skill, or honing soft skills such as communication and leadership, building skills enhances a person's confidence, competence, and overall ability to tackle challenges. In a fast-paced and competitive environment, continuously building skills is essential for staying relevant, excelling in one's career, and pursuing one's passions. Here are two ways you can do this:

- **Skill development:** Engage in activities that develop your skills and competencies. This could be through education, hobbies, or new experiences. The more you develop yourself, the more confident you will be when performing tasks that require these exact skills. There are always new skills to learn, so keep up with the new era and sign yourself up for some great skills courses.

- **Continuous learning:** Adopt a mindset of lifelong learning. The pursuit of knowledge and skills enhances self-efficacy and self-esteem. As long as you keep the desire alive to always want to learn and grow, you will always remain confident in yourself.

Social Connections

The relationships you share with the people around you are very important. How you interact with others, as well as the status of your social life, all play a role in either making or breaking your self-esteem. Now, it's a given you won't get along with just anyone as we all have our preferences when it comes to building friendships and relationships; however, it's crucial to build strong social networks in life. You can enhance social connections by focusing on these two aspects:

- **Supportive relationships:** Surround yourself with people who uplift and support you. Positive relationships reinforce self-worth.

- **Community involvement:** Engage in community or group activities that foster a sense of belonging and purpose.

Cultivating Self-Compassion

Cultivating self-compassion is crucial for maintaining mental and emotional well-being. Showing kindness and understanding toward oneself in times of struggle or failure can help reduce negative self-talk, self-criticism, and feelings of inadequacy. By practicing self-compassion, individuals develop resilience, self-acceptance, and a healthier relationship with themselves. This mindset allows for greater self-care, self-forgiveness, and the ability to navigate life's challenges with greater ease and grace. Ultimately, fostering self-compassion can lead to improved overall mental health, enhanced self-esteem, and a more positive outlook on life. Here are some tips on how you can cultivate self-compassion in your life.

Practicing Self-Kindness

- Gentle self-treatment: Treat yourself with the same kindness and understanding as you would a friend. This involves recognizing when you are suffering and responding with care.

- Supportive self-talk: Use compassionate language when talking to yourself, especially during times of failure or difficulty. Even if no one else will, you should be the one to pick yourself up from failure and try again.

Mindfulness

- Present-moment awareness: Practice mindfulness to stay present and aware of your thoughts and emotions without judgment. This helps in acknowledging pain and suffering without getting overwhelmed.

- Nonjudgmental stance: Accept your imperfections and mistakes without harsh judgment. Mindfulness helps in viewing these experiences as part of personal growth.

Self-Compassion Exercises

- Loving-kindness meditation: Once again, meditation proves to be beneficial. Engage in loving-kindness meditation to cultivate feelings of warmth and care toward yourself and others.

- Compassionate letter writing: Write letters to yourself from a compassionate perspective, addressing your struggles and offering words of comfort and understanding. Sometimes, all you need is to give yourself that love you so desperately want.

Overcoming Self-Criticism

- Identifying negative self-talk: Being more aware of the thoughts that go through your mind, which are negative in nature, can help you overcome self-criticism.

- Awareness: Become aware of critical thoughts and their triggers. Understanding when and why self-criticism arises is the first step in addressing it.

- Journaling: Keep a journal to track self-critical thoughts and patterns. This can help in identifying specific areas where self-criticism is most prevalent.

Challenging Negative Beliefs

- Cognitive restructuring: CBT to the rescue once again! You can use cognitive-behavioral techniques to face your challenges and question them head-on. Then, you can also restructure negative beliefs. Ask yourself for evidence against these beliefs and consider alternative, more positive interpretations.

- Reality testing: Question the validity of your self-critical thoughts. Are they based on facts or assumptions? Replace them with balanced, realistic thoughts. Refuse to listen to thoughts that have no basis or proof.

Reframing Failures

- Learning opportunities: View failures as opportunities for growth and learning rather than reflections of self-worth. This shift in perspective reduces the sting of failure and encourages resilience.

- Growth mindset: Embrace a growth mindset, which emphasizes improvement and learning over inherent ability. This mindset fosters resilience and reduces self-criticism.

Self-Compassionate Responses

- Respond with compassion: When self-critical thoughts arise, respond with compassionate statements. Remind yourself that making mistakes is part of being human and does not diminish your worth.

- Self-compassion breaks: Take self-compassion breaks during stressful times. Pause, acknowledge your suffering, and offer yourself kindness and understanding in the moment.

Building a Support Network

Having a strong support network can be like wrapping yourself in a cozy blanket on a chilly day—it provides a comforting space where you can freely share your thoughts and emotions. When those moments of overthinking arise, having caring friends, family members, or mental health professionals to lean on can bring a sense of clarity, comfort, and validation. Here are the advantages of having a support network:

- Buffer against stress: A strong support network provides emotional cushioning, which reduces the mental burden and helps prevent overthinking.

- Perspective and clarity: Friends and family can offer different perspectives, helping to clarify situations and reduce the tendency to ruminate.

- Emotional ventilation: Sharing thoughts and feelings with others helps release pent-up emotions, alleviating the pressure that contributes to overthinking.

Types of Support: Emotional, Informational, and Practical

Support can be broken down into three categories: emotional, informational, and practical. Looking at support from these perspectives will help you identify the *value-adding* people in your life.

- Emotional support involves offering empathy, care, and reassurance. This form of support helps individuals feel valued and understood, which can reduce feelings of isolation and anxiety.

- Informational support includes advice, suggestions, and information that can help solve problems or make decisions. This can reduce uncertainty and the tendency to overthink.

- Practical support involves providing tangible assistance, such as helping with tasks, running errands, or providing financial support. This can alleviate the stress of overwhelming responsibilities, reducing the need to overthink solutions.

Cultivating Meaningful Relationships

Quality over quantity in friendships. It's more beneficial to have a few deep, meaningful relationships than numerous superficial ones. Quality friendships provide genuine support and understanding. This results in less doubt and less overthinking. Yes, it can be difficult to find authentic people whom you can trust, but you can use the following strategies to help you build strong relationships with people:

- Active listening: Practice active listening by being fully present in conversations, showing empathy, and responding thoughtfully. This strengthens bonds and fosters mutual understanding.

- Regular communication: Maintain regular contact with friends and family. Consistent communication nurtures relationships and demonstrates care and commitment.

- Shared experiences: Engage in activities and experiences together. Shared experiences create lasting memories and strengthen emotional bonds.

- Expressing appreciation: Show appreciation and gratitude for your friends and family. Acknowledging their support reinforces positive relationships and encourages reciprocation.

Seeking Professional Help

There are instances where you could be left feeling defeated even after trying all the strategies and tips provided to you. In this case, it would be wise to consider seeking help from a professional. There is a stereotype attached to the idea of people seeking help from psychologists and therapists, and this often demotivates people from reaching out for help. Nevertheless, asking for help is the best decision you can make for yourself and your loved ones. Don't be held back by any stereotypes that mislead the truth. Here's how you can identify when it's time to seek help professionally:

- Persistent overthinking: If overthinking persists despite self-help strategies, professional help may be necessary. Therapy can provide targeted interventions to address underlying issues.

- Emotional distress: When overthinking leads to significant emotional distress, anxiety, or depression, therapy can offer structured support and coping mechanisms.

- Poor coping skills: When you lose the ability to cope with the responsibilities in your life, and you begin to slack. Therapy can enhance coping skills, helping individuals manage stress and reduce overthinking.

Different Types of Professional Support

- Cognitive behavioral therapy (CBT): CBT therapists help clients identify and change negative thought patterns and behaviors that contribute to overthinking.

- Support groups: Group therapy and support groups provide a communal space to share experiences and gain insights from others facing similar challenges.

- Psychiatrists and psychologists: For severe cases, psychiatrists and psychologists can provide comprehensive mental health care, including medication and intensive therapy.

- Life coaches and counselors: Life coaches and counselors can offer guidance and support for personal and professional challenges, helping to reduce stress and overthinking.

Community and Group Activities

Engaging in community groups or activities is an effective form of therapy that gives you a sense of purpose. You can join these groups online or visit local community centers. Here are the benefits of joining community groups:

- Sense of belonging: Participating in community groups fosters a sense of belonging and social connectedness, which can reduce feelings of isolation and overthinking.

- Shared interests: Engaging in activities with people who share similar interests creates opportunities for meaningful connections and support networks.

- Mutual support: Shared interests provide common ground for forming supportive relationships where individuals can offer and receive help.

- Reduced loneliness: Regular social interaction combats loneliness and promotes a positive outlook, which can mitigate the tendency to overthink.

- Increased well-being: Participation in group activities has been shown to improve overall well-being, reducing stress and enhancing life satisfaction.

Segue

What an insightful chapter, right? A chapter focused on strategies, tools, and tips that have been designed to help you annihilate your overthinking problem. You learned about building emotional resilience and support networks, self-compassion, CBT, and much more. It's vital that you put into practice everything you learned in this chapter.

Chapter 5:

Lifestyle Changes for a Calmer Mind

Change is painful, but nothing is as painful as staying stuck somewhere you don't belong. –Mandy Hale

Changing Your Habits, Changing Your Mindset!

This chapter is all about encouraging and motivating you to pursue a mindset change. From here on out, the only thing left for you to do is put your plan into action and overcome your bad overthinking. The only way this is possible is if you change your mindset and your habits.

Healthy Lifestyle Choices

Meet Martha, a woman of wisdom at 44, celebrated for her thoughtful and thorough approach to life. While her career and personal pursuits thrived, Martha often found herself entangled in a web of worry and self-doubt. Despite her success, true peace and joy eluded her. There came a day when Martha realized her overthinking took a toll not only on her mind but also on her body. It was a pivotal moment that sparked her decision to embrace healthier habits and a more uplifting outlook.

Her journey began with simple yet powerful changes. Martha embraced a daily ritual of gentle movement, taking serene morning strolls and finding solace in evening yoga sessions. The gentle rhythm of exercise became her sanctuary, relieving the weight of stress and anxiety. Paying keen attention to her nourishment, Martha welcomed a diet brimming with vitality—abundant in fresh fruits, vegetables, and wholesome grains. By bidding adieu to processed foods, her body responded with newfound vigor and radiance.

Furthermore, Martha shifted her internal dialogue, choreographing a dance of positivity to challenge her inner critic. Whenever the shadows of overthinking loomed, she paused to draw deep breaths, guiding her thoughts toward gratitude and hope. As her journey flourished, Martha felt a profound transformation within. The tendrils of anxiety loosened their grip, and she blossomed with newfound confidence and tranquility. Martha learned to release the need for control, embracing each moment with open-hearted acceptance.

How to Develop a Healthy Lifestyle

In today's fast-paced world, taking care of your health and staying fit are more important than ever. It's not just about feeling good physically but also boosting your mental well-being and productivity and reducing the risk of chronic diseases. With unhealthy eating habits on the rise, it's crucial to prioritize your health and fitness for a balanced and fulfilling life. Making time for regular exercise, eating well, and getting enough rest are essential steps to achieving and maintaining optimal health in today's society. Here are some great ways you can start living a healthier lifestyle.

Regular Physical Exercise

Exercise is one of the most important aspects of maintaining good health. Not everyone is a fan of exercise, mostly because we don't understand that all the work that goes into it makes a huge difference actually to our bodies. Here's how regular physical exercise can help you:

- **Reduces stress hormones:** Exercise lowers cortisol levels and increases endorphins, improving mood and overall well-being. When you are highly stressed, you can hit the gym and blow off some steam while performing some high-intensity workouts. However, this only works if you make it a habit and not something you do once in a while.

- **Shifts your focus:** Exercise provides a healthy distraction from anxious thoughts and promotes a state of relaxation. Activities like yoga and tai chi combine physical movement with mindfulness, enhancing both physical and mental well-being. When overthinking sets in, you can use these strategically designed exercises to help you divert your attention to a state of peace and calm.

- **Improves sleep quality:** Physical activity helps regulate sleep patterns, which can reduce nighttime overthinking. When you keep yourself active, you are using up your energy in the right avenues, so by the time you go to bed, you will be in a better position to have a good rest.

- **Boosts mental health:** Regular exercise is linked to reduced anxiety and depression, providing a natural way to manage overthinking. When you feel good in your body, you will feel good in your mind. Being fit boosts self-confidence, which in turn promotes a positive self-image as well.

Exercises That Help Eradicate Overthinking

Engaging in physical exercises can be a great way to help manage overthinking and promote mental well-being. Here are some exercises that can specifically help with calming an overactive mind:

- **Yoga:** Yoga combines physical postures with breath work and meditation, promoting relaxation and mindfulness. Poses like Child's Pose, Corpse Pose, and

Forward Fold can help quiet the mind and reduce stress and anxiety.

- **Tai chi:** This gentle form of exercise focuses on slow, flowing movements and deep breathing, which can help center the mind, improve focus, and reduce mental clutter.

- **Walking or jogging:** Going for a walk or a jog outdoors can help clear your mind, boost your mood, and release endorphins. The rhythmic motion of walking or jogging can be meditative and provide a distraction from overthinking.

- **Dance:** Dancing is a fun and expressive way to release tension and shift your focus away from repetitive thoughts. You can dance freely to your favorite music or follow along with a dance workout video.

- **Swimming:** Swimming is a great exercise that can be both low-impact and fast-paced. It can also be invigorating and calming. The rhythmic nature of swimming, combined with the focus on breathing, can help quiet the mind and promote relaxation.

- **Martial arts:** Practicing martial arts like karate or tae kwon do can help channel excess energy and promote mental discipline. The focus on technique and mindfulness in martial arts can help quiet the mind and improve concentration.

Remember to listen to your body and choose activities that you enjoy and that make you feel good. Regularly incorporating physical exercise into your routine can be a valuable tool in managing overthinking and promoting overall mental well-being.

Healthy Eating Habits

We all love food, especially comfort food like ice cream, fried chips, and chocolates. We particularly enjoy these foods when we are stressed or feeling emotional, as they help us feel better instantly. However, unhealthy eating habits can cause serious health issues in people of all ages. As part of living a healthy lifestyle, you must also eat healthily to ensure you are giving your mind and body everything they need to thrive. Here are the benefits of eating healthily:

- Supports brain function: Proper nutrition provides the brain with essential nutrients that support cognitive function and mood regulation. Foods like almonds, fish, and various vegetables are great for improving brain health and strengthening your mind.

- Regulates energy levels: Eating regular, balanced meals helps maintain steady energy levels, reducing the likelihood of fatigue-induced overthinking. If you eat too much or too little, it can have an adverse impact on your energy levels. Maintaining balance is key to disciplining your mind and body against overthinking.

- Reduces inflammation: Anti-inflammatory foods can improve overall mental health. Foods like olive oil, spinach, nuts, berries, peppers, and certain fish all double as anti-inflammatory agents, which are great for your body.

Healthy Sleeping Habits

Getting a good night's sleep is like giving your body a big warm hug of rejuvenation! During sleep, your body works hard to repair tissues, organize memories, balance hormones, and boost cognitive function. It's a key ingredient in supporting your immune system, lifting your mood, and gearing you up for a productive day ahead. Remember, skimping on sleep can open the door to health challenges like obesity, diabetes, and heart disease, so tuck in and prioritize those Z's for a healthier, happier you! Here's how sleep can help you become a better version of yourself:

- Enhances cognitive function: Adequate sleep is essential for optimal brain function, reducing the likelihood of overthinking. When you are more alert and aware, you can identify triggers and patterns that come with an episode of overthinking.

- Regulates emotions: Proper sleep helps stabilize mood and reduces stress. Have you ever seen anyone in a good mood when they didn't have a good night's sleep? My guess is your answer is a "No." This is because sleep aids in overcoming both mental and physical fatigue, and this promotes healthy emotional regulation.

- Improves concentration: Quality sleep enhances focus and productivity. Whether it's your career, business venture, hobby, or anything else, if you want to be successful in any aspect of life, you must be focused and productive.

Hobbies and Interests

Hobbies and interests are crucial for maintaining mental well-being, reducing stress, and promoting personal fulfillment. They provide a healthy outlet for creativity, relaxation, and self-expression and can also help individuals connect with like-minded people and build social networks. Engaging in hobbies and interests outside work or daily responsibilities can improve the overall quality of life and contribute to a balanced and fulfilling lifestyle. Here's how having hobbies can help you mentally and emotionally:

- Distracts from overthinking: Focusing on hobbies provides a mental break from negative thoughts.

- Boosts mood: Doing something enjoyable can improve your overall mood and reduce stress.

- Promotes creativity: Engaging in creative activities can stimulate the mind and provide a sense of accomplishment.

When people participate in activities that bring joy and fulfillment, they rarely fall into episodes of overthinking. This is why you should always look for new ways to keep yourself busy and fulfilled.

Practical Tips for Developing Healthy Habits

Healthy habits are the type of habits that people should keep for life, but they aren't easy to develop, and this can be quite a challenge for some. Below are some tips to help you develop these healthy habits and maintain them in the long run:

- Set realistic goals: Start with small, achievable goals to build momentum. This is the first step to training your mind to get into the groove of developing habit-forming behaviors.

- Be consistent: Regular practice is key to making habits stick. If you create a routine for yourself, you will be able to fall into these healthy habits much easier. Consistency requires a certain level of dedication as well, so if you are not committed to the process, you will not be able to develop these healthy habits.

- Track progress: Keep a journal or use apps to monitor your habits and progress. The modern age has made it possible to track almost anything from your smartphone, iPad, or computer. This will help you determine where you are falling short so you can take action early on to prevent failure.

- Seek accountability: Share your goals with friends or family for support and accountability. When people are aware of the positive changes you are making in your life, they tend to keep an eye on you to make sure you are staying in line. This can help you stay motivated.

- Be patient: Building new habits takes time, so be patient with yourself. Don't be too hard on yourself when you do not achieve certain goals within a desired time frame as long as you learn from your mistakes and make better choices going forward.

Digital Detox and Managing Technology Use

Oh, isn't it amazing how technology can easily influence our tendency to overthink? With its constant stream of information, social media updates, and communication tools, it can sometimes flood our minds. Those never-ending notifications, the always-on connectivity, and the endless sea of content can easily lead to feeling overwhelmed, comparing ourselves to others, and getting lost in our thoughts. All this can escalate our overthinking, making us feel more anxious and stressed, finding it hard to stay present in the moment. It's so important to be mindful of how we use technology and set boundaries to ensure it doesn't add to our overthinking and negatively impact our mental well-being. Let's take a closer look at how technology can fuel overthinking:

- Information overload: Constant access to information through smartphones, computers, and other devices can overwhelm the brain, leading to mental fatigue and overthinking.

- Social media: The perpetual comparison on social media platforms can lead to anxiety and self-doubt, fostering a habit of overanalyzing one's own life in comparison to others.

- 24-7 connectivity: The expectation of being constantly available and responsive to emails, messages, and notifications can create stress and disrupt relaxation time, leading to persistent overthinking.

- Disruption of sleep patterns: Exposure to blue light from screens before bedtime can interfere with sleep quality, making the mind more susceptible to overthinking.

Ricardo's Story

Ricardo was a 30-year-old man who found himself constantly struggling with overthinking due to his obsession with social media. What started as a harmless way to stay connected with friends and family had turned into a toxic habit that consumed his every waking moment. Every time Ricardo posted a picture or a status update, he would anxiously check for likes and comments, his self-worth hinging on the validation he received online. The pressure to present a perfect image of his life led to excessive filtering and editing, slowly eroding his self-esteem.

Comparing himself to carefully curated images of others on social media only fueled his insecurities. The fear of missing out, coupled with the constant showing off from acquaintances and strangers, left him feeling inadequate and lonely. As Ricardo scrolled through his feed, he often found himself caught in a downward spiral of negative thoughts. He would overanalyze every post, wondering if he had said the right thing or if his life measured up to those around him. The fear of judgment from others paralyzed him, making him second-guess even the most mundane decisions.

Despite his rational mind knowing the disconnect between online personas and reality, Ricardo couldn't shake off the need for approval and validation from his virtual audience. The dopamine hits from likes and comments provided fleeting moments of happiness, but they were always overshadowed by a sense of emptiness and dissatisfaction. He would lie in bed at night wondering if anyone would ever like him for who he was or if they were just interested in the social media version of Ricardo. There were too many thoughts circling around in his mind, and it only got worse each time Ricardo scrolled through his social media apps.

Setting Boundaries With Digital Devices

Now that you understand how technology can encourage overthinking, some measures need to be taken to deal with this issue. The first thing you have to do is put boundaries in place to curb this problem. Setting boundaries is a great way to ensure you not only reduce the risk of triggering your overthinking but also set healthy habits when it comes to device usage. Here are some tips to help you set these boundaries:

- Designate tech-free zones: Create areas in your home where technology use is restricted, such as the bedroom or dining area, to encourage more meaningful interactions with your family and friends offline. This also promotes relaxation and rest.

- Schedule screen time: Schedule dedicated times during the day for reviewing emails, engaging with social media, and participating in other digital tasks. Utilize applications or the inherent functionalities on your devices to establish time constraints.

- Turn off Nonessential notifications: Disable notifications for nonessential apps to reduce distractions and the urge to constantly check your device. Sometimes, these notifications distract you and lure you to open those apps and start scrolling, for example, online shopping adverts.

- Practice the 20-20-20 rule: With this rule, every 20 minutes you spend on the screen, take a 20-second break to look at something 20 ft away. This can reduce eye strain and mental fatigue. When you spend too much time in front of the screen, it will damage your eyes and cause discomfort, not forgetting the headaches you could experience because of mental fatigue.

- Unplug before bedtime: Establish a digital curfew at least an hour before bed. Engage in relaxing activities like reading a book, taking a bath, or practicing meditation instead. This soothes your mind and body and gets you in the mood for a good night's rest, so when you wake up in the morning, you feel more rejuvenated.

Techniques for a Successful Digital Detox

- Set clear goals: Define what you hope to achieve from a digital detox, such as reducing stress, improving focus, or spending more quality time with loved ones.

- Start small: Begin with short periods of detox, such as a few hours each day, and gradually increase the duration. This makes the process less daunting and more manageable.

- Engage in offline activities: Rediscover hobbies and activities that do not involve screens, such as reading, gardening, hiking, or cooking. Physical activities, in particular, can be very effective in reducing stress and overthinking.

- Use digital detox apps: Apps can help track and limit your screen time, encouraging more mindful use of technology.

- Stay accountable: Share your detox plans with friends or family members. Having a support system can provide encouragement and make it easier to stick to your goals.

- Reflect and adjust: After a detox period, reflect on how you felt and any changes in your mental state. Adjust your technology use habits based on what worked and what didn't.

Time Management and Organization

Effective time management and organization play a crucial role in reducing overthinking by offering a structured approach to daily tasks and responsibilities. When individuals allocate their time efficiently and organize their activities, they create a clear roadmap for accomplishing goals, which can alleviate feelings of overwhelm and uncertainty. By prioritizing tasks, setting deadlines, and creating schedules, individuals can break down complex projects into manageable steps, making them less daunting. This structured approach not only enhances productivity but also fosters a sense of control and empowerment over one's workload.

Furthermore, effective time management allows individuals to allocate dedicated time for relaxation, self-care, and reflection, which are essential for mental well-being. By creating a balance between work and personal life, individuals can prevent burnout and reduce the tendency to ruminate excessively on past events or worry about the future. Overall, by implementing strategies for effective time management and organization, individuals can cultivate a more focused and balanced mindset, ultimately reducing overthinking and promoting mental clarity and peace of mind.

Prioritizing Tasks and Avoiding Procrastination

Prioritizing tasks is important because it helps individuals focus their time and energy on activities that are most important and urgent. Here are some key reasons why prioritizing tasks is crucial:

- Efficiency: Prioritizing tasks allows individuals to identify and tackle high-priority tasks first, ensuring that important deadlines are met and critical objectives are achieved. This approach helps prevent wasted time and resources on less important or nonurgent tasks.

- Time management: By prioritizing tasks, individuals can allocate their time effectively and ensure they are working on the most important projects or activities at any given time. This helps in managing workload effectively and avoiding last-minute rushes or procrastination.

- Stress reduction: Prioritizing tasks helps individuals feel more in control of their workload, reducing feelings of overwhelm and stress. By focusing on key priorities, individuals can prevent tasks from piling up and avoid the anxiety that comes with juggling multiple responsibilities simultaneously.

- Goal achievement: Prioritizing tasks ensures that individuals are making progress toward their goals and objectives. By identifying and prioritizing tasks that align with their long-term objectives, they can stay focused on what truly matters and make meaningful strides toward success.

- Resource allocation: Prioritizing tasks helps individuals allocate their resources, such as time, energy, and attention, effectively. By focusing on high-priority tasks, people can optimize their resources and maximize their productivity.

You can use two methods to help you rank your tasks in order of importance: the Eisenhower Matrix and the ABC method. Each one is explained as follows:

- **Eisenhower Matrix:** Organizes tasks into four quadrants based on urgency and importance: urgent and important, important but not urgent, urgent but not important, and neither urgent nor important. Focus on important tasks to avoid last-minute stress, but don't forget that the *neither urgent nor important* tasks still need your attention at some point to avoid procrastination.

- **ABC method:** Rank tasks as A (must do), B (should do), and C (nice to do). This helps in focusing on high-priority activities first. This method makes life incredibly easier, particularly when it comes to prioritizing tasks that are work-related.

Time Management Techniques

- Time blocking: Set aside specific amounts of time for different tasks or activities throughout the day. This reduces decision fatigue and ensures dedicated focus periods. Give yourself a set amount of time to make decisions to avoid overanalyzing. Trust your instincts and move forward once the time is up.

- Pomodoro Technique: Work in short, focused intervals—typically 25 minutes—followed by a 5-minute break. After 4 intervals, take a longer break. This method helps maintain concentration and prevents burnout.

- Daily planning: Start each day with a plan. Use tools like to-do lists, planners, or digital apps to outline your tasks and schedule. Review and adjust your plan as needed.

- Decluttering your physical and mental space: A clean and organized workspace can reduce distractions and promote a clear mind. Regularly declutter and organize your physical and digital spaces.

- Calendars and planners: Use physical or digital calendars to keep track of appointments, deadlines, and events.

Establishing daily routines can provide a sense of stability and predictability, reducing the cognitive load of constant decision-making. Include morning and evening routines to start and end your day calmly. Large tasks can feel overwhelming and lead to overthinking. Break them down into smaller, manageable steps to make progress feel more achievable.

Segue

In conclusion, the interconnection between a healthy mind and body is undeniable. By prioritizing both physical and mental well-being, individuals can achieve a harmonious balance that promotes overall health and vitality. Taking care of one's body through regular exercise, nourishing nutrition, and adequate rest, alongside practicing mindfulness, stress management, and seeking support when needed, can lead to a more fulfilling and joyful life. Remember, a healthy mind and body go hand in hand, and investing in both is key to living a vibrant and flourishing life.

Chapter 6:

Maintaining Progress and

Dealing With Relapse

Life is very interesting… in the end, some of your greatest pains become your greatest strengths. –Drew Barrymore

Staying Strong on Your Journey

This chapter will help you understand the importance of maintaining your progress and staying committed to your journey. Overthinking is a habit that can always take root again, but only if you allow it. In this chapter, you will learn how to stay focused and also deal with relapse when it happens.

Maintaining Your Progress

As we have discussed earlier in this book, overthinking often goes unnoticed, and it could have been very well established during your early adolescent years. This is quite a long time to have a habit that you are blissfully unaware of. Nevertheless, now that you are serious about overcoming your bad overthinking, you have to take the necessary measures to maintain your progress. Below, we discuss a few strategies that will aid you in keeping your eye on the goal.

Maintaining progress and preventing relapse when dealing with overthinking involves a combination of strategies aimed at both short-term relief and long-term habit changes. You need to remember that falling back into overthinking patterns does not make you a failure. Here are some amazing tips for you:

- Boundaries with your thoughts: Grant yourself some dedicated time to process your thoughts and worries, but also set boundaries to prevent excessive rumination and overanalysis. Consider scheduling a special *worry time* each day to address your concerns.

- Self-care magic: Nestle into the warmth of self-care by tending to your physical, emotional, and mental well-being. Engaging in activities that bring you joy, relaxation, and fulfillment can work wonders in reducing stress and nurturing a brighter mindset.

- Sprinkle gratitude: Envelop yourself in the goodness of life by focusing on the positive aspects and cultivating a sense of gratitude. Whether it's keeping a gratitude journal or simply reflecting on what you're thankful for, this practice can help shift your perspective and ease overthinking.

Remember, the journey of overcoming overthinking is a gentle process that unfolds with time and practice. Shower yourself with patience and celebrate each little victory along the way. Be kind to yourself as you traverse the path toward maintaining your progress. Always remember that everyone's path is different. Just because something worked for someone else does not mean it will work for you. You've got this!

Encountering Relapse

Mona's Story

Meet Mona, a 32-year-old working mom who has faced a long and challenging battle with overthinking. For years, she found herself trapped in a cycle of constant worrying and rumination, which eventually took a toll on her mental health, leading to depression. The weight of her relentless thoughts clouded her days, making it hard for her to find peace. Determined to reclaim her mental well-being, Mona embarked on a journey to overcome her overthinking. Through therapy, self-reflection, and implementing mindfulness practices, she slowly started to untangle the knots of anxious thoughts that had consumed her mind. With each small step forward, she felt a glimmer of hope and a sense of empowerment.

However, despite her progress, Mona faced a setback along her path. Life's challenges and stressors triggered a relapse, plunging her back into the familiar grip of overthinking. She found herself battling the same old patterns and feelings of despair that she thought she had left behind. Yet, Mona refused to give up. Recognizing that setbacks are a natural part of any transformative journey, she showed courage and resilience by picking herself up once again. With renewed determination, she restarted her journey to conquer overthinking, this time armed with the wisdom gained from her past struggles.

Mona learned to be kind to herself, celebrate her progress no matter how small, and seek support from loved ones when needed. She understood that overcoming overthinking is not a linear path but a winding road with ups and downs. As Mona navigated through the peaks and valleys of her mental health journey, she discovered a newfound strength within herself. Each setback became a lesson, and each relapse a stepping stone toward growth. With perseverance and self-love, Mona continued her journey, determined to find peace of mind and inner calm.

Mona's story is a testament to the resilience of the human spirit and the power of self-care and self-compassion in overcoming challenges. It serves as a reminder that healing is a nonlinear process, and it's okay to stumble on the way as long as you keep moving forward.

Dealing With Relapse

As you have gathered from the above story about Mona, relapse is a part of the journey. Overthinking is a habit, an addiction of some sort that keeps tugging at you trying to get you to turn back. Yes, it's very difficult to recover from a relapse; however, it's not impossible. If you are determined enough, you will stand up each time you fall. Don't hold a relapse against yourself. Understand that failure is a stepping stone to success. Below are some strategies that will help you arise from your relapse stronger than before.

Acknowledging the Relapse

It's crucial to acknowledge and accept that relapses are a natural part of the process of change. Instead of being harsh on yourself, view a relapse as an opportunity for growth and self-discovery. Understand that setbacks are common in any journey toward personal development and use this experience to gain insights into your triggers and responses.

Identifying Triggers

Reflect on what factors might have triggered your relapse. Was it a specific event, a prolonged period of stress, or certain thought patterns that resurfaced? By pinpointing your triggers, you can better anticipate and manage them in the future. Understanding what sets off your overthinking can empower you to develop effective coping strategies.

The journey of our minds can sometimes be nudged toward overthinking by unseen triggers. We have elaborated on these triggers earlier in this book; however, they will be briefly reiterated below to help you understand them:

- Stress and anxiety: When waves of stress and anxiety wash over us, it's natural for our thoughts to wander into overdrive.

- Perfectionism: As we strive for excellence in every facet of our lives, the pursuit of flawlessness can lead us down a path of deep contemplation.

- Traumatic experiences: Past trials and tribulations can act as echoes in our minds, triggering moments of deep contemplation as we seek to make sense of troubling memories.

- Fear of failure: The haunting fear of failure or the weight of making the wrong choices can provoke bouts of overthinking.

- Lack of confidence: If the seeds of self-doubt and insecurity take root, they can blossom into overthinking. Constantly questioning our capabilities and wavering in self-assurance can lead us to dissect situations with a fine-tooth comb.

- Overload of information: The deluge of data can overwhelm our senses, sparking a whirlwind of contemplation.

- Rumination: Dwelling incessantly on unresolved matters can create a loop of deep introspection.

It's a gentle reminder to acknowledge these stirrings and embrace strategies to gently guide your thoughts. By tending to the roots of these patterns, you pave the way for a serene and harmonious mind.

Revisiting Coping Strategies

Return to the coping mechanisms that have proven effective for you in the past. Whether it's mindfulness practices, meditation, cognitive-behavioral techniques, or other tools, reapply these strategies to regain control over your thoughts and emotions. Consistency in using these methods can help you navigate through challenging times and regain stability.

Practicing Self-Compassion

During a relapse, it's crucial to practice self-compassion and kindness toward yourself. Embracing self-compassion can help you navigate through difficult times with greater resilience and understanding.

Setting Small Goals

Rather than aiming to eliminate overthinking altogether, focus on setting small, achievable goals. Concentrate on reducing the duration or intensity of your overthinking episodes. Celebrate incremental victories to build momentum and reinforce positive behaviors. By breaking down your goals into manageable steps, you can make progress toward overcoming overthinking in a more attainable and sustainable way.

Seeking Professional Help

If you find that relapses are frequent, overwhelming, or impacting your daily life significantly, consider seeking help from a therapist or counselor. Professional mental health support can provide you with tailored guidance, coping strategies, and techniques to address your specific needs. A trained professional can offer valuable insights and support to help you navigate through relapses and work toward long-term mental well-being. Remember, seeking help is a sign of strength and a proactive step toward healing and growth.

If someone finds themself struggling after a setback on their path to overcoming overthinking, there are various caring professionals ready to offer support:

- **Therapists:** Skilled in cognitive behavioral therapy (CBT), therapists can compassionately help individuals work through negative thought patterns, develop coping strategies, and embrace mindfulness to ease overthinking.

- **Psychologists:** Understanding and empathetic psychologists provide therapy and guidance to help unravel the causes of overthinking and create healthier coping mechanisms.

- **Psychiatrists:** When overthinking is intertwined with anxiety or other mental health concerns, a psychiatrist can evaluate symptoms and offer medication assistance if needed.

- **Support groups:** Connecting with others facing similar challenges in support groups can bring a sense of belonging and comfort. Sharing experiences and support among peers can be incredibly uplifting.

- **Life coaches or counselors:** Offering a gentle hand, life coaches can provide direction and tools to help individuals navigate overthinking and progress in their personal or professional lives.

- **Online therapy:** Accessible online therapy platforms provide a convenient way to receive professional support for overthinking.

Reflect and Learn

After you've managed the relapse, take some time to reflect on what you've learned from the experience. Understanding why it happened and how you overcame it can make you more resilient in the future. In the battlefield of life, as you face a defeat or setback, remember that reflecting on it is crucial for your development and evolution. Here are battle-tested strategies to assist you in reflecting on a failure or setback:

1. **Conquer your emotions:** Embrace the fury and disappointment that defeat brings. Allow yourself to feel the anger, frustration, and sorrow. Conquering these emotions is the initial triumph toward your rebirth.

2. **Analyze the enemy:** Retreat and observe the battleground with a sharp eye. Identify the weaknesses that led to your downfall. Whether it was your own actions, treacherous circumstances, or unforeseen challenges, acknowledge them with precision.

3. **Extract wisdom from the battle:** Instead of surrendering to despair, pillage the battlefield for lessons. Evaluate the tactics that succeeded and those that failed. Arm yourself with this knowledge to fortify your strategy for future conquests.

4. **Forge new battle plans:** Forge new battle plans fortified by the wisdom gained from your reflections. Set ambitious yet attainable objectives that incorporate the lessons learned from the setback. Draft a battle scheme with decisive actions to surge forward triumphantly.

5. **Show yourself mercy:** Show yourself mercy as you undergo this grim process. Understand that defeats are as much a part of the warrior's path as victories.

Embrace these setbacks as opportunities for growth and transformation.

6. **Rally your comrades:** Rally your trusted allies—friends, mentors, or counselors—and enlighten them on your struggles. Seek their counsel and support as you navigate through the trials of reflection. Their guidance will be your beacon in the midst of the chaos.

7. **Fix your sight on the present:** While it is vital to scrutinize the battles lost, do not languish in the shadows of past defeats. Fix your gaze on the present campaign and the maneuvers required to advance toward your objectives.

By approaching the reflection process with the spirit of a seasoned warrior, ready to learn and adapt, you can turn each defeat into a formidable lesson that propels you toward boundless victories on the battlefield of life.

Success Stories

Even though success can have different meanings for different people, no one can be successful without hard work and goals. You must have something tangible to work toward, or else your journey will be one that is baseless and fruitless. Here are some success stories from people who have dealt with overthinking in their own way and found what works best for them. Let their experiences and journeys shine a light on your situation so that you can find hope in your darkest hour.

Claire's Confession

Hello there, I'm Claire, and I'm on a journey as a recovering overthinker.

Let me share a bit about what that means. For a long time, I found myself caught in a cycle of constantly analyzing what others thought of me. It consumed a significant part of my life. However, the moment I realized that all that energy spent on overthinking wasn't serving me well, everything started to change for the better.

People like us, the overthinkers, often have a deep sense of empathy and passion. While these qualities are amazing, sometimes our focus on others' perceptions can overshadow our own accomplishments. It can hold us back, making us dwell on conversations, second-guessing ourselves instead of embracing the positive contributions we bring. Overthinking can create anxiety and hinder our growth by making us fear failure rather than see opportunities to learn.

While there are countless self-help books claiming to cure overthinking, I call bluff on that. I believe that being an overthinker is a part of who we are. Instead of trying to eliminate it, we can learn to leverage it as a strength rather than a weakness. In a recent coaching session, I helped someone who wanted to *defeat* overthinking. The truth is, you can't defeat it entirely. However, you can learn to channel your overthinking in a positive direction and avoid letting it spiral into stress.

It's not the act of overthinking itself that causes stress; it's the content of our thoughts during those moments. I still find myself caring too much about things that shouldn't occupy my mind—like other people's opinions or small conversations.

When I catch myself overthinking these days, I ask myself three simple questions:

1. Why am I investing my energy in this thought? Is it worth it?

2. Will this matter in six months?

3. Do I have clear evidence to support my thoughts, or am I assuming things?

You may never fully rid yourself of overthinking, but you can certainly manage it and prevent it from controlling you.

Here are some insights I've gathered as a recovering overthinker:

1. We overthink not because we're insecure, but because we tend to think a lot—about everything.

2. Our caring nature can sometimes backfire when we feel responsible for others' feelings.

3. Sleep can be challenging when our minds decide to replay the day's events on a loop.

4. Despite its downsides, overthinking can lead to innovative ideas and problem-solving.

5. Overthinking may manifest more strongly in certain areas of our lives, depending on where our insecurities lie.

In a world overflowing with information and constant communication, mastering our overthinking tendencies and building resilience is crucial (*Confessions of a Recovering Overthinker*, 2020).

Paul's Story

I am a 29-year-old man, married with 2 young children, currently employed as a teacher at a remarkable independent school in Australia. My initial encounter with anxiety took place roughly 4 years ago during a whirlwind phase of my life. In just a span of a few months, I went through a series of significant life events—losing and finding a job, getting married, selling and buying a house, and traveling extensively.

Despite the apparent positivity of these events, the stress they brought along was overwhelming and unforeseen. As the wedding approached, I started experiencing peculiar symptoms—a loss of appetite, a sense of disconnection from the world, and a perpetual feeling of impending doom. The most distressing moment occurred when my wife walked down the aisle. Although I knew I loved her and should have felt happy, I found myself standing there like an empty vessel, unable to genuinely connect with my emotions.

This unsettling experience propelled me into a sudden and alarming bout of anxiety. I became fixated on my emotions and appetite and sought answers tirelessly on the internet. Looking back, I now realize the toll my relentless pursuit of a diagnosis and cure took on my mental and physical well-being.

I experimented with countless *cures*, convinced that each one would hold the key to my recovery. I consulted numerous medical professionals, tried various supplements, medications, and lifestyle changes, and spent endless hours scouring the internet for solutions. Despite my efforts, I continued to traverse through a state of depersonalization, enveloped in irrational thoughts and a sense of detachment from reality.

It was only after a friend recommended a book to me that I began to see a glimmer of hope. Initially skeptical, I eventually embraced the process of healing, gradually learning to shift my focus from negative thoughts to positive affirmations. Through speaking to my mind as if it were a separate entity, I started to regain control over my thoughts and emotions.

Though setbacks were part of the journey, a significant turning point came with the birth of my daughter. Holding her for the first time, I experienced a wave of genuine emotion, shedding tears of relief and joy. At that moment, I realized that the real me, buried under layers of anxiety, was finally resurfacing. Sharing this profound moment with my wife, who had been a pillar of support throughout my struggle, marked a significant milestone in my healing process.

Anangsha's Story

Growing up, I used to have a severe addiction: overthinking. When I was younger, I worried too much about simple things like handing over an assignment to a teacher or saying hello to a new friend. As I grew older, this manifested itself in more severe forms, like agonizing over what college to pick and spending hours debating whether or not adding a certain degree to my name would add any value to my life.

When I started my business, this addiction got worse. Whenever I got a new business idea, I thought of possible scenarios in which I might fail. I ran over the cons of the new venture so many times in my mind that by the time I sat to take some action, all my motivation was gone. None of these business ventures ever saw the light of day. But this post isn't about those failures. This post is about how I managed to end my addiction. It was possible only because of this story of a village visited by *death*.

One day, a farmer ventured out of his village to try his luck.

After walking for a few hours, he came across a fast-flowing river with a narrow bridge. He was frightened, knowing he could never make it to the other end alive. He didn't want to die here but was reluctant to turn back.

Then, he saw someone already standing near the bridge.

The man was hooded in complete black. He had red eyes and no smile. When he came closer, the farmer realized the stranger was *death* itself.

Terrified, he was sure these were his last few moments on the planet.

But Death just let out a hollow laugh and said, "Beware, O Human. Before the sun rises tomorrow, I will visit your village and take 50 of your people."

The man was scared beyond words. He ran back home and shared the sad news with his folks. The entire village was in a state of shock and dismay as they went to sleep.

The next day, almost 500 people were dead.

The farmer felt a sense of betrayal.

He rushed toward the same river to meet Death and demand back his friends' lives.

Death was waiting for him at the same spot. Laughing, Death enquired, "I see, Human. You have come here again. What brings you to me?"

Shaking with fear and rage, the farmer shouted, "You had foretold you'd take 50 of my village men, but you took 500. What did those poor men do to deserve such wrath?"

Death's reply shocked the man, "Oh, but I took only 50, human. Worry took the rest."

What can you learn from Death's story?

Stop overthinking. The outcomes are not in your control. Most of what happens in life is a game of chance. The more you show up and give your best, the better your chances of making it big. After all, you can't hope to win the lottery if you never buy the ticket, right? Don't waste precious time overthinking and overanalyzing every aspect of your decision. Take action (Alammyan, 2023).

Positive Affirmations for Overcoming Overthinking

You are your biggest supporter. There is no one else who knows you better than you know yourself. So, who better to motivate and encourage you than yourself? Positivity is powerful, especially when it comes to shifting mindsets. You can change your entire thought process just by uttering words of hope and love into your life. Below, you will find 20 positive affirmations that will help you get started on your journey to overcoming your bad overthinking:

1. I am in control of my thoughts, and I choose to focus on the present moment.

2. I trust in my ability to handle whatever challenges come my way.

3. I release the need to overanalyze every situation and trust in the process of life.

4. I am capable of finding solutions to any problems that arise.

5. I deserve peace of mind, and I let go of unnecessary worries.

6. I embrace uncertainty as an opportunity for growth and learning.

7. I am enough just as I am, and I do not need to constantly doubt myself.

8. I cultivate a positive mindset by focusing on what I can control.

9. I choose to let go of negative thoughts and replace them with empowering beliefs.

10. I am resilient, and I bounce back from setbacks with renewed strength.

11. I accept that it is okay to not have all the answers right now.

12. I am grateful for the present moment and all the blessings in my life.

13. I trust my intuition to guide me in making decisions with confidence.

14. I give myself permission to take breaks and practice self-care when needed.

15. I acknowledge that overthinking does not serve me, and I choose to release this habit.

16. I am worthy of love, happiness, and peace of mind.

17. I believe in my ability to persevere through challenges and come out stronger.

18. I choose to focus on what is within my control and let go of what is not.

19. I embrace imperfection as a part of being human and learn to be gentle with myself.

20. I am deserving of inner peace, and I trust in my ability to overcome overthinking.

Segue

Out of all the chapters in this book, this one is the most important. The reason being is that staying motivated and dedicated to your journey is harder than you might think. True work starts when you are going through the process and faced with many challenges that throw you off course. Your true strength shows when you hit rock bottom because it will either push you to become better or knock the wind out of you. Use the advice given in this chapter to help you persevere on your journey. You are stronger than you could ever imagine!

Conclusion

Dear friend, you have reached the end of your journey with this book; however, your journey to setting yourself free from overthinking is just beginning. Looking back on everything you have learned, would you now say that you are more confident in your capabilities to give yourself a better life? Do you have a newfound trust in yourself that you didn't have before? I hope your answers are a yes to each of these questions! You probably learned a lot while reading this guide, and you understand what it takes to revamp and become the best version of yourself.

Look, the steps you have to take aren't easy, especially when you are trying to break old habits. There will be times when you will feel like you are wasting your time. You will feel stuck, and you might even resort to overthinking all over again. But you have to understand that this is part of the process. Each time, you will only get better and better at curbing your overthinking. That dark, gloomy cloud of thoughts will no longer cause a storm within your mind. You are in charge of your sunshine. You have the power to calm the storm and shift the clouds. But you can only do this if you equip yourself with the tools and strategies highlighted in this book.

By exploring strategies such as mindfulness, cognitive restructuring, meditation, journaling, keeping yourself busy with fulfilling activities, and self-compassion, you can gain the tools you need to take control of your thoughts and live a more present and fulfilling life. It is possible to break free from the suffocating grips of overthinking and cultivate a mindset of peace, clarity, and resilience. Embrace these tools, practice self-awareness, and trust in your ability to overcome overthinking. Remember, no one knows you better than you know yourself.

The power to change lies within you. You just have to find what works best for you and run with it. All the best on your journey, and don't forget to always believe in yourself!

Glossary

Catastrophizing: Exaggerating your difficulties or thinking you are in a worse situation than you really are.

CBT: Cognitive behavior(al) therapy.

MCBT: Mindfulness cognitive behavioral therapy.

Neuroticism: A negative personality trait that involves an individual feeling many different negative emotions.

OCD: Obsessive-compulsive disorder.

PTSD: Post-traumatic stress disorder.

Relapse: Falling back into a former state after a period of improvement.

Ruminating: Going over the same thoughts in one's mind again and again.

References

Acosta, K. (2022, January 11). *What causes overthinking—and 6 ways to stop.* Forbes Health. https://www.forbes.com/health/mind/what-causes-overthinking-and-6-ways-to-stop/

Alammyan, A. (2023, January 29). *A story about death that helped me overcome overthinking.* Anangsha Alammyan. https://www.anangsha.me/a-story-about-death-that-helped-me-overcome-overthinking/

Are you an overthinker? (n.d.). Psychology Today. https://www.psychologytoday.com/intl/blog/the-runaway-mind/202001/are-you-an-overthinker

aware.ae. (2021, September 5). *The nine different types of overthinking.* Aware. https://aware-ae.com/the-different-types-of-overthinking/

Cherry, K. (2023, November 2). *What is cognitive behavioral therapy (CBT)?* Verywell Mind. https://www.verywellmind.com/what-is-cognitive-behavior-therapy-2795747

Confessions of a recovering overthinker. (2020, September 30). Circle In. https://circlein.com/confessions-of-a-recovering-overthinker/

Gadye, L. (2018, June 29). *What part of the brain deals with anxiety? What can brains affected by anxiety tell us?* Brainfacts.

https://www.brainfacts.org/Diseases-and-
Disorders/Mental-Health/2018/What-part-of-the-
brain-deals-with-anxiety-What-can-brains-affected-by-
anxiety-tell-us-062918

Gottberg, K. (2016, April 8). *Mindfulness – the cure for a busy and overthinking mind.* SMART Living 365. https://www.smartliving365.com/mindfulness-cure-busy-overthinking-mind/

Herrity, J. (2023, February 4). *120 uplifting quotes about change.* Indeed. https://www.indeed.com/career-advice/career-development/quotes-about-chang

McGee, K. (2023, March 16). *Can you inherit anxiety?* GoodRx. https://www.goodrx.com/health-topic/anxiety-disorders/is-anxiety-genetic-or-hereditary

McGough, N. B. (2024, February 2). *61 quotes about strength and resilience for uncertain times.* Southern Living. https://www.southernliving.com/culture/quotes-about-strength

Otte, C. (2011). Cognitive behavioral therapy in anxiety disorders: Current state of the evidence. *Dialogues in Clinical Neuroscience, 13*(4), 413–421. https://www.ncbi.nlm.nih.gov/pmc/articles/PMC3263389/

Team, H. (2023, November 22). *Catastrophizing: What it really means and how to stop it.* Heal Your Nervous System. https://healyournervoussystem.com/catastrophizing/#

The mind maze: How overthinking affects your mental health. (n.d.). Strategies for Success.

https://www.strategiesforsuccessaz.com/blog/the-mind-maze-how-overthinking-affects-your-mental-health

Wignall, N. (2021, February 17). *7 psychological reasons you overthink everything.* Nick Wignall. https://nickwignall.com/7-psychological-reasons-you-overthink-everything/

Image References

Akyurt, E. (2019, January 21). *Person holding heart shaped cut out* [Image]. Pexels. https://www.pexels.com/photo/person-holding-heart-shaped-cut-out-1820525/

Borba, J. (2019, August 29). *Brown human eye* [Image]. Pexels. https://www.pexels.com/photo/brown-human-eye-2873058/

Cottonbro studio. (2020, June 29). *Woman in a black tank top wearing black boxing gloves* [Image]. Pexels. https://www.pexels.com/photo/woman-in-black-tank-top-wearing-black-boxing-gloves-4753923/

Dapo, O. (2019, December 6). *Man wearing black headset* [Image]. Pexels. https://www.pexels.com/photo/man-wearing-black-headset-3345882/

Inturi, P. (2018, April 28). *Silhouette of a man at daytime* [Image]. Pexels. https://www.pexels.com/photo/silhouette-of-man-at-daytime-1051838/

Mendez, J. (2018, October 25). *Smiling woman looking upright standing against yellow wall* [Image]. Pexels. https://www.pexels.com/photo/smiling-woman-looking-upright-standing-against-yellow-wall-1536619/

Odintsov, R. (2020, June 3). *Man with arms outstretched admiring the view from mountain* [Image]. Pexels. https://www.pexels.com/photo/man-with-arms-outstretched-admiring-view-from-mountain-cliff-4552990/

Patrascu, L. (2022, June 28). *Silhouette of a man near a red light* [Image]. Pexels. https://www.pexels.com/photo/silhouette-of-a-man-near-a-red-light-12633374/

Piacquadio, A. (2018, March 15). *Photo of a woman thinking* [Image]. Pexels. https://www.pexels.com/photo/photo-of-a-woman-thinking-941555/

Pixabay. (2016a, October 22). *Woman wearing white, pink, and green floral dress holding pink bougainvillea flowers* [Image]. Pexels. https://www.pexels.com/photo/woman-wearing-white-pink-and-green-floral-dress-holding-pink-bougainvillea-flowers-206557/

Pixabay. (2016b, December 20). *Chess piece* [Image]. Pexels. https://www.pexels.com/photo/chess-piece-260024/

Pixabay. (2017, March 20). *Clear light bulb* [Image]. Pexels. https://www.pexels.com/photo/clear-light-bulb-355948/

Pwinicki, M. (2022, July 24). *White and yellow fireworks in the sky* [Image]. Pexels. https://www.pexels.com/photo/white-and-yellow-fireworks-in-the-sky-12966761/

Sayles, B. (2018, June 28). *Photo of a man thinking* [Image]. Pexels. https://www.pexels.com/photo/grayscale-photo-of-man-thinking-in-front-of-analog-wall-clock-1194196/

Stock project, R. (2020, November 27). *A man covering his ears* [Image]. Pexels. https://www.pexels.com/photo/a-man-covering-his-ears-6003315/

Sun, L. (2019, March 9). *Man working out* [Image]. Pexels. https://www.pexels.com/photo/man-working-out-2294361/

Tankilavich, P. (2020, August 31). *Women having conversation while looking at each other* [Image]. Pexels. https://www.pexels.com/photo/women-having-conversation-while-looking-at-each-other-5234582/

Tran, B. (2017, October 29). *Inspirational quotes written on a planner* [Image]. Pexels. https://www.pexels.com/photo/inspirational-quotes-written-on-a-planner-636237/

Wei, W. (2018, December 3). *Assorted vegetables* [Image]. Pexels. https://www.pexels.com/photo/assorted-vegetables-1656666/

Winkler, M. (2023, December 25). *The word fight is spelled out on tiles* [Image]. Pexels. https://www.pexels.com/photo/the-word-fight-is-spelled-out-in-scrabble-tiles-18500864/

Made in United States
Troutdale, OR
11/24/2024

25212275R00097